Recipes from the Moon

RECIPES
from the
MOON

More Recipes from the Horn of the Moon Cafe

Gary Beardsworth

TEN SPEED PRESS
Berkeley, California

TEN SPEED PRESS
P.O. Box 7123
Berkeley, CA 94707

Cover design by Margery Cantor
Text design by Tasha Hall
Illustrations by Kathleen Edwards

Library of Congress Cataloging-in-Publication Data

Beardsworth, Gary.
    Recipes from the Moon / Gary Beardsworth
        p.   cm.
    Includes index.
    ISBN 0-89815-681-5
    1. Horn of the Moon Cafe (Montpelier, Vt.)
    2. Vegetarian cookery.   3. Cookery—Vermont—
Montpelier.   I. Horn of the Moon Cafe (Montpelier, Vt.)   II. Title.
    TX837.B371995
    641.5'097434—dc20   94-38000
                                                CIP

FIRST PRINTING 1995
Printed in the United States of America
2 3 4 5 — 99 98 97 96 95

*This book is dedicated to my wife, Rhonda, and
my children, Jesse, Erin, Niko, and Ethan.
Not only were they guinea pigs, they were
creators, supporters, experimenters, and critics.*

I couldn't have done it without you.

This cookbook owes its life to the many people who have supported the Horn of the Moon Cafe over the past years, both as employees and as customers and friends. I couldn't hope to name them all, but they know who they are.

Thank You.

<u>Contents</u>

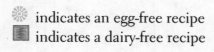 indicates an egg-free recipe
 indicates a dairy-free recipe

Contents

Contents

Introduction

THE HORN OF THE MOON CAFE OPENED in Montpelier, Vermont in 1977, and moved to its present location on Langdon Street, overlooking the North Branch of the Winooski River, two years later. The original owner, Ginny Callan, decided to sell the cafe 13 years later so that she could devote more time to her young family. My wife Rhonda and I purchased the cafe from Ginny in July 1990.

I had been a frustrated bureaucrat working for the city of Montpelier for many years when we learned that the Horn of the Moon Cafe was for sale. My wife and I had been vegetarians since the early 1970s for both moral and practical reasons. I had put myself through college working in restaurants, learning and doing almost everything that there is to do in a restaurant kitchen, and I had often thought about going back into the business. As a vegetarian, however, I was uncomfortable working in a traditional food service environment, which is largely based on the preparation of meat. The Horn of the Moon Cafe seemed like a business that we could do without having to compromise our values. So, we took the plunge.

The $4^{1}/_{2}$ years that we have owned the cafe have been challenging. The recession that began in the early '90s greatly affected our sales and caused us to look at new ways of doing things. We have practiced some creative job consolidation to cut staff and to utilize the special talents of various employees. We have found more efficient ways of doing things. We continue to recycle all of our glass, steel cans, plastic jugs, newspapers, and corrugated cardboard. We experimented with composting our food waste in a small area right behind the cafe to further reduce the amount of material we sent to the landfill. (According to the Central Vermont Regional Planning Commission, this was one of a very small number of commercial urban composting experiments in the United States.) Unfortunately, we found that composting so close to our back door caused problems with odors and flies, so we discontinued our operation after two years. We still try to send our compostables to other people who have a use for them.

With all of the challenges of running a cafe, why have we written a cookbook? The first *Horn of the Moon Cookbook*, written by Ginny Callan and published in 1987 (Harper Collins), continues to sell well. People from all parts of the country who have the cookbook come into the cafe when they are visiting in the area. We receive many calls every year from people interested in buying a copy of the cookbook or asking about a particular recipe from the book that they are in the process of making. We are also frequently asked if a meal that a customer has enjoyed at the cafe is in the cookbook. Often the recipe is not there simply because eight years have gone by since that cookbook was written and we are constantly trying new things.

We have become more concerned, as have many of our customers, with lowering the fat and cholesterol in the meals we serve. This cookbook is filled with new recipes that have been successful at the cafe. We have also tried to offer a larger selection of egg-free and/or dairy-free meals for those who are trying to cut back or eliminate these foods from their diet. (In this book, egg-free recipes are indicated by a ☀ ; dairy-free recipes by a ▦ .) What we have not done, and will not do, is what many other vegetarian restaurants have chosen to do: serve animal foods. I believe that we are the oldest remaining vegetarian restaurant in New England, and possibly a much larger area, that has stayed true to its original philosophy of not serving meat, fish, or fowl.

Ingredients

WE HAVE TRIED TO INCLUDE RECIPES which use ingredients which can easily be found in a natural foods store or a good natural foods section of a large grocery store. If we feel that an ingredient may be difficult for you to find, we have tried to offer an alternative. Wherever possible, we use organic rather than commercial food products because we believe that they are a healthier, more natural choice and do not contribute to the myriad ecological problems caused by modern agribusiness farming techniques. Cost, unfortunately, is a necessary consideration in the restaurant business, making the use of some commercial food products inevitable. In general, the commercial foods we use fall into two groups: Canned and frozen vegetables which are not available organically in large, commercial containers; and small quantities (less than a case) of fresh fruits and vegetables. However, because some products are difficult to find, don't hesitate to make substitutions, if necessary.

With a few exceptions, we use only natural sweeteners in our dishes, primarily honey, maple syrup and Sucanat® (a granular sweetener made from organic sugar cane juice with a light molasses taste). Some customers still cringe at the thought of honey or Sucanat® in their coffee, however, and so for them we provide white sugar. We also use white and brown sugar in one of our most popular desserts, chocolate chip cookies, but also offer a cookie made with honey, Sucanat®, and malt-sweetened chocolate chips.

We use only organic dried beans in our recipes, most commonly pintos, kidneys, black turtle, baby limas, chick-peas, navy beans, lentils, and green and yellow split peas. All beans, especially organic ones, should be carefully picked over to remove any pebbles or other foreign material. We do this by pouring the beans out onto a large baking sheet and checking through them. Be sure to rinse the beans well after sorting.

Some of the harder beans, such as chick-peas and pintos, should be soaked before cooking to shorten their cooking time. Either soak the beans overnight, or bring them to a boil, then turn off the heat and let the beans sit, covered, for 1 hour. Bring the beans back to a simmer and finish cooking. All of this is unnecessary if you have a pressure cooker, which will cook most beans in 1 hour or less. Some beans, especially soy and chick-peas, foam a lot when cooked and should not be cooked in a pressure cooker.

We use only commonly available cheeses in our recipes (Cheddar, Swiss, mozzarella, parmesan). With the exception of Parmesan, all of our cheese is rennetless. Rennet is an enzyme used to produce cheese that comes from cow's stomach. Fortunately for us who care, vegetable and microbial alternatives are available and widely used.

Any recipe, no matter how good, can be improved. Sometimes the smallest change can make a good recipe great. If you make a change to a recipe, write it in the cookbook. Do it in pencil so you can change it later if you need to. Don't rely on your memory to adjust a recipe the same way each time you make it. If you make larger or smaller quantities than the recipe calls for, write the new amounts in the margin so you don't have to recalculate the amounts each time. Most importantly, don't be afraid to experiment. If you don't have one or two of the ingredients called for in a recipe, look around your kitchen to see if you have something comparable to use in replacement. *Be creative.*

Recipes from the Moon

Breakfast Dishes

Cinnamon–Vanilla French Toast

Serves 4

French toast is a favorite food on our breakfast menu. We serve it with butter and maple syrup.

4 eggs, beaten
$^1/_4$ cup heavy (whipping) cream or
    half-and-half
$^1/_4$ teaspoon vanilla extract

$^1/_2$ teaspoon ground cinnamon
$^1/_4$ teaspoon ground nutmeg
8 slices whole-wheat, raisin, or
    French bread, sliced 1-inch thick

In a shallow glass baking dish, beat eggs, cream or half-and-half, vanilla, and spices well. Dip the bread briefly in the batter to coat both sides. Cook the bread on a hot, oiled griddle or in a hot, oiled cast-iron pan until brown on both sides. Serve immediately.

AMARETTO FRENCH TOAST

Replace the spices and vanilla with 3 to 4 tablespoons Amaretto and cook as directed.

 ## Cashew French Toast

Serves 4

This is our egg- and dairy-free French toast, for our customers who do not eat eggs or dairy products.

$^1/_2$ cup (2 ounces) cashews
$^1/_4$ cup hulled sunflower seeds
$^1/_4$ cup sesame seeds
1 teaspoon vanilla extract
$1^1/_4$ cups plain soy milk or more, as needed

8 ounces tofu
2 tablespoons honey
$^1/_2$ teaspoon ground cinnamon
$^1/_2$ teaspoon ground nutmeg
8 slices whole-wheat, raisin, or French bread, sliced 1-inch thick

Bake the cashews on a baking sheet in a preheated 350°F oven for 5 minutes, or until they are lightly browned. Grind the cashews, sunflower seeds, and sesame seeds in a blender or food processor. Add all the remaining ingredients except the bread and blend, adding more soy milk if necessary to make a batter about the consistency of pancake batter. Pour the batter into a shallow dish. Dip the bread into the batter to coat both sides, and cook it on a hot, oiled griddle or a hot, oiled cast-iron pan until browned on both sides. (NOTE: This batter is much stiffer than ordinary French toast batter. Use care when taking the bread out of the batter to keep it from tearing and falling apart.)

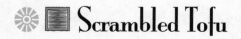 ## Scrambled Tofu

Serves 4

This is a great breakfast alternative to eggs. On many mornings, we serve more scrambled tofu than scrambled eggs at the cafe.

16 ounces firm tofu, mashed
½ cup nutritional yeast
1 teaspoon black pepper
3 tablespoons tamari sauce or soy sauce

In a medium bowl, mash the tofu with a fork. Stir in the nutritional yeast and pepper. Add tamari or soy sauce and mix again. Cook on a hot, oiled griddle or in a hot, oiled cast-iron skillet until browned, stirring frequently.

Spicy Scrambled Tofu

Substitute 1 to 2 teaspoons crushed red pepper flakes for the black pepper in the preceding recipe.

Honey–Wheat Germ Pancakes

Serves 4

I may be biased, but I think these pancakes are the best. They are also egg-free. If you prefer eggs in your pancakes, substitute 2 eggs for the 2 tablespoons yogurt in the recipe.

½ cup raw wheat germ
2 cups whole-wheat pastry flour
⅔ cup unbleached all-purpose flour
4 teaspoons baking powder
1 teaspoon salt
3 tablespoons canola or other mild vegetable oil
3 tablespoons honey
2 tablespoons plain yogurt
2½ to 3 cups milk

Mix wheat germ, flours, baking powder, and salt together in a medium bowl. In another medium bowl, mix the oil, honey, and yogurt together and beat until well mixed. Blend in the milk. Stir the liquid ingredients into the dry ingredients just until mixed. Let sit for 5 minutes. Spoon batter onto a hot, oiled griddle or cast-iron skillet. When bubbles begin to form on the top of the pancakes, turn and cook on the other side for 1 to 2 minutes.

 ## Granola

Makes 16 cups

Granola is not a big seller at the cafe, but we don't seem to be able to keep it around the house. It is a popular snack with our children, either plain or with yogurt or milk. This recipe makes a lot, but it stores well in the freezer.

4 cups rolled oats

2 cups wheat flakes

1½ cups rye flakes

1 cup raw wheat germ

2 cups dried flaked coconut

2 cups (8 ounces) walnuts (my son says these are optional)

½ cup canola or other mild vegetable oil

¾ cup maple syrup or half maple syrup and half honey mixture

¼ teaspoon salt

¼ teaspoon cider vinegar

¾ tablespoon vanilla extract

3 cups raisins or currants

Preheat the oven to 350°F. In a large bowl, combine the oats, wheat and rye flakes, wheat germ, coconut, and walnuts. In a small saucepan, combine oil, maple syrup or syrup-honey mixture, salt, and vinegar, and bring to a boil. Remove from heat and stir in the vanilla. Pour this mixture over the grain mixture and mix until the grains are well coated. Spread evenly no more than 1½ inches deep in baking pans. Bake for about 45 minutes, or until golden, stirring every 10 to 15 minutes to prevent burning. (The thinner the grain mixture is spread on the baking pans, the faster it will cook.) Return the granola to the bowl you used to mix it in and let it cool briefly. Stir in the raisins.

Gallo Pinto

Serves 4

Steve, a friend and former waitperson at the cafe, brought us this recipe from Central America. We serve it as a special at the cafe when we have spicy black beans left over from black bean tostadas.

$^1/_2$ cup brown rice
1 cup lightly salted water
3 cups Spicy Black Beans (page 50)
2 teaspoons canola or other mild vegetable oil
1 small red onion, diced

1 red bell pepper, seeds and membranes removed, diced
2 teaspoons minced fresh cilantro (optional)
8 eggs, poached or fried

In a small saucepan, bring the water to a boil and add the rice. Lower heat, cover, and simmer for 45 to 50 minutes, or until the rice is tender and the water is absorbed. Mix the rice into the black beans. Add cilantro. In a small sauté pan or skillet, heat the oil and sauté the onions and pepper for 5 minutes. Place equal amounts of the rice and bean mixture on 4 plates. Spread the onions and pepper over the beans. Top with 2 eggs per plate and serve.

Eggs Florentine

Serves 4

2 tablespoons butter, plus more for buttering muffins
2 tablespoons unbleached all-purpose flour
$^1/_2$ cup milk, or more as needed
$^1/_2$ cup (2 ounces) grated Cheddar cheese

1 tablespoon vinegar
4 cups packed spinach leaves
4 English muffins
8 eggs
Pinch of paprika

To make the cheese sauce: Melt the butter in a small saucepan. Stir in the flour until it bubbles; stir and cook for 1 minute. Gradually add the milk while stirring. Add the grated cheese and stir until melted. Add additional milk if the sauce is too thick to spoon easily over the eggs. Do not let the sauce boil.

To make the English muffins: Place 2 inches of water and the vinegar in a large sauté pan or skillet and bring to a boil. Meanwhile, cook the spinach until wilted, about 3 minutes, in a medium saucepan with a little water. Drain excess water. Begin toasting the English muffins. Crack the eggs into boiling water, keeping them as far apart as possible so they won't cook together. Butter the muffins when toasted and place a small amount of steamed spinach on each half. Remove the eggs from the pan with a slotted spoon and place 1 on top of each muffin half. Cover the eggs with the cheese sauce and sprinkle lightly with paprika. Serve immediately. (For a quick version of this recipe, sprinkle grated Cheddar cheese on top of eggs in place of the cheese sauce.)

POACHED EGGS WITH ASPARAGUS SPEARS AND CHEESE SAUCE

Follow the recipe for Eggs Florentine, but substitute Swiss cheese for the Cheddar cheese. Substitute 12 asparagus spears, steamed until crisp-tender, about 6 minutes, for the spinach.

Soups

MANY PEOPLE COME TO THE CAFE just because of our soups. Most of our soups are thick and hearty and make a meal in themselves. We always have at least two soups to choose from, plus chili and miso. In the winter we try to have one dairy and one nondairy soup, but in the summer we tend to avoid dairy soups altogether.

❉ ▣ Monterey Chowder

Makes 12 cups

The recipe for this soup originally called for butter, milk, and cheese, but we always made a dairy-free version for those who preferred it that way. Before long we found that we liked the dairy-free version better and stopped making the dairy version altogether.

2 cups dried lima beans

8 cups water

3 tablespoons canola or other mild vegetable oil

1/2 bunch celery, chopped

1 large onion, chopped (2 cups)

2 red or green bell peppers, seeds and membranes removed, chopped

4 large garlic cloves, minced

1 jalapeño chili, minced

4 tablespoons dried dillweed

1 1/2 to 2 cups fresh or thawed frozen corn kernels

One 16-ounce can crushed tomatoes

5 to 6 fresh tomatoes, chopped (4 cups), or two 16-ounce cans diced tomatoes

1 to 1 1/2 teaspoons salt

3/4 teaspoon pepper

Place the lima beans and water in a large saucepan and bring the water to a boil. Reduce heat to a simmer and cook until tender, about 2 hours. Heat oil in a soup pot over medium heat and sauté the celery, onions, red or green peppers, garlic, jalapeños, and dill until crisp-tender, about 10 minutes. Add the cooked lima beans, corn, and tomatoes to the soup pot and simmer for about 30 minutes. Add salt and pepper in small increments, as necessary, to season.

✳ Potato Soup

Makes 12 cups

Potato soup is one of the quickest and easiest soups to make. We make it at home frequently when we are in a hurry and need a quick meal that everyone likes.

5 to 6 unpeeled potatoes (4 cups), cut into 1/4-inch dice
1 large onion, chopped (2 cups)
1 cup chopped celery
5 cups water
2 teaspoons salt

1/2 teaspoon pepper
4 tablespoons butter
1/4 cup unbleached all-purpose flour
1/2 cup heavy (whipping) cream or 1 cup milk
Milk to thin soup, if necessary

Place the diced potatoes, onions, and celery in a soup pot with the water. Bring the water to a boil, reduce heat to a simmer, and cook until the potatoes are done, about 10 minutes. Add the salt and pepper and mash the potatoes slightly with a potato masher (or blend a portion of the potatoes, onions, and celery in a blender or food processor and add it back to the pot).

Melt the butter in a small pan over low heat. Stir the flour into the butter until the mixture bubbles. Continue cooking and stirring for 1 minute. Add this mixture to the soup and mix well. Add the cream or milk. Add milk if the soup is too thick and adjust the seasoning. Do not let the soup boil after the milk has been added or the soup will separate.

❊ Potato–Dill Soup

Makes 12 cups

The variation of the preceding potato soup is seasoned with parsley and dill.

5 cups water
5 to 6 unpeeled potatoes (4 cups), cut into $1/4$-inch dice
1 large onion, chopped (2 cups)
1 cup chopped celery
$1/2$ cup minced fresh parsley
$1/4$ cup dried dillweed

$1/2$ cup (1 stick) butter
$1/4$ cup unbleached all-purpose flour
$1/2$ cup heavy (whipping) cream or 1 cup milk
4 teaspoons salt
1 teaspoon pepper
Milk to thin soup, if necessary

Place the diced potatoes in a large pot. Add the water and bring to a boil. Reduce heat to simmering, add the chopped onions and celery, and cook until the potatoes are tender, about 10 minutes. Add the parsley and dill. Mash some of the potatoes in the soup with a potato masher, or blend some of the potatoes, onions, and celery in a blender or food processor, then return the purée to the pot.

In a small saucepan over low heat, melt the butter and stir in the flour until the mixture bubbles, then cook and stir for 1 minute more. Stir this mixture into the soup. Add the cream or milk, salt, and pepper. Thin the soup with milk, if desired. Do not let the soup come to a boil after adding the cream or milk.

❊ Sour Cream–Potato Soup

Makes 12 cups

This soup may be served either hot or cold. If serving cold, add additional milk and adjust the seasoning after chilling.

5 to 6 cups unpeeled potatoes
  (4 cups), cut into $1/4$-inch dice
1 large onion, chopped (2 cups)
1 cup chopped celery
$1/4$ cup (1 stick) butter
$1/4$ cup unbleached all-purpose flour

$1\,1/4$ cups sour cream
$1/2$ cup heavy (whipping) cream or
  1 cup milk
4 teaspoons salt
1 teaspoon pepper
Milk to thin soup, if necessary

Place the potatoes, onions, celery, and water in a large soup pot. Bring the water to a boil, reduce to a simmer, and cook until the potatoes are done, about 10 minutes. Mash some of the potatoes in the soup pot with a masher to make the soup creamier (or blend some of the soup in a blender and return it to the pot). Melt the butter in a small pan and add the flour; stir until the mixture bubbles. Cook and stir 1 minute longer, then add to the soup. Add the sour cream, cream or milk, salt, and pepper. Thin with milk, if desired. Do not let the soup boil after adding the cream.

❋ Potato–Broccoli Soup

Makes 12 cups

5 cups water
5 to 6 unpeeled potatoes (4 cups), cut
  into $1/4$-inch dice
1 tablespoon canola or other mild
  vegetable oil
1 large onion, chopped (2 cups)
4 stalks broccoli, chopped (4 cups)
1 teaspoon dried dillweed

$1/4$ cup (1 stick) butter
$1/4$ cup unbleached all-purpose flour
$1/2$ cup heavy (whipping) cream or
  1 cup milk
1 tablespoon salt
1 teaspoon pepper
Milk to thin soup, if necessary

Place the potatoes in a soup pot with water. Bring to a boil, reduce heat, and cook until the potatoes are tender, about 10 minutes. Heat the oil in a large sauté pan or skillet and cook the onions until they become translucent, about 10 minutes. Add the broccoli and dillweed and continue cooking until the broccoli is cooked but still crisp, about 5 minutes. When the potatoes are done, mash them in the soup pot or blend to make a creamier soup. Add the broccoli and onions. Melt the butter in a small saucepan over low heat. Stir in the flour until it bubbles and cook for 1 minute. Stir this mixture into the soup. Stir in cream or milk, salt, and pepper. Do not let the soup boil. Thin the soup with milk, if necessary.

✳ Carrot Chowder

Makes 8 cups

We originally called this Cream of Carrot Soup. Paul, one of our regular lunch customers, told us that it wasn't soup, it was chowder. We think he's right.

15 large carrots, washed or peeled and grated (6 cups)

4 tablespoons ($^1/_2$ stick) butter

2 large onions, cut into $^1/_4$-inch dice (4 cups)

2 medium potatoes, cut into $^1/_4$-inch dice (1$^1/_2$ cups)

2 to 3 teaspoons salt

1 tablespoon canola or other mild vegetable oil

1 tablespoon honey

2$^1/_2$ cups water

$^1/_4$ cup unbleached all-purpose flour

1 cup heavy (whipping) cream or 1 cup milk

$^1/_2$ teaspoon paprika

$^1/_2$ teaspoon black pepper

$^1/_4$ teaspoon cayenne pepper

Milk to thin soup, if necessary

Grate 12 of the carrots (you should have about 6 cups) and cut the remaining carrots into half-moon slices (you should have 1$^1/_2$ to 2 cups). Heat the oil in a large soup pot and sauté the onions and carrots until the onions are translucent, about 10 minutes. Add the potatoes, salt, honey, and water, and cook until the potatoes are done, about 30 minutes. Melt the butter in a small saucepan over low heat. Stir the flour into the butter until it bubbles, then cook and stir for 1 minute. Stir this mixture into the hot soup. Add the cream or milk, paprika, black pepper, and cayenne, and heat over low heat. Do not let the soup boil. If the soup is too thick, add milk until the desired consistency is reached.

Chili

Makes 10 cups

Our chili uses seitan and cilantro, which add interesting tastes and texture. Even without them, this is a hearty main-course dish.

1 cup dried kidney beans, or one 16-ounce can

1 cup dried pinto beans, or one 16-ounce can

3 to 4 tablespoons olive oil or vegetable oil

1 large onion, chopped (2 cups)

5 garlic cloves, minced

1 1/2 to 2 green bell peppers, seeds and membranes removed, chopped

1/2 to 1 tablespoon jalapeño chili, minced

1 teaspoon whole or ground cumin seed

1 1/2 teaspoons dried basil

1/2 teaspoon dried coriander

2 1/2 teaspoons chili powder

1 teaspoon salt

Pinch of cayenne pepper

1 tablespoon minced fresh cilantro (optional)

1 cup fresh or thawed frozen corn kernels

One 28-ounce can crushed tomatoes

1 fresh tomato, diced

4 ounces seitan, cut into 1/4-inch dice (optional)

Pick over the beans for pebbles, and rinse. Soak the beans overnight, if possible, in a large saucepan with 6 cups water. The next day, add more water, if necessary, to cover beans by about 1 inch. Bring to a boil, lower heat to a simmer, and cook for about 2 hours, covered, or until the beans are tender. (Kidney beans cook slightly faster than pintos, so you may want to soak the beans separately and add the kidney beans 30 minutes after starting the pinto beans.) If you don't have time to presoak the beans, cook them in 6 cups of water for 2 1/2 to 3 hours. As the beans cook, make sure that they are always covered with water.

Heat the oil in a large sauté pan or skillet over medium heat and sauté the onions, garlic, bell peppers, and jalapeños until onions are translucent, about 10 minutes. Add the cumin, basil, coriander, chili powder, salt, cayenne, and cilantro.

Add the cooked beans to the sautéed vegetables. Add the corn, tomatoes, and seitan, and cook briefly over low heat until heated through.

❊ Greek Spinach Soup

Serves 8

This is another experiment that worked. I needed a dairy soup but didn't want to make one of our regular ones. I remembered a popular soup that one of our former cooks had made with spinach, feta, and yogurt. This was my attempt to recreate that soup.

8 cups lightly salted water
1 pound fresh spinach, stemmed, or
   one 10-ounce package frozen
   spinach, thawed
1 cup finely chopped onions
4 garlic cloves, minced
2 medium potatoes, diced (2 cups)
4 tablespoons butter
1/4 cup whole-wheat pastry flour or
   unbleached all-purpose flour

1/2 cup sour cream
1/3 cup plain yogurt
4 ounces feta cheese, crumbled
   (1 cup)
2 tablespoons fresh lemon juice
1/2 tablespoon pepper
2 to 3 teaspoons salt

Bring the water to a boil in a large soup pot. Add the onions, garlic, and potatoes, and cook until the potatoes are tender, about 10 minutes. Mash the potatoes partially with a potato masher, or blend some of them in a blender or food processor and return the purée to the pot. Stir in the spinach. In a small saucepan, melt the butter over low heat. Stir the flour into the butter until it bubbles, then cook and stir for 1 minute. Add this mixture to the hot soup. Stir in the sour cream, yogurt, feta, lemon juice, pepper, and 2 teaspoons salt. Let the soup simmer for 10 to 15 minutes and add more salt as needed. Do not let the soup boil.

 Gazpacho

Makes 8 cups

Prepare this mildly spicy and very refreshing cold soup in advance, if you can, as the taste improves as the flavors are allowed to blend.

One 16-ounce can diced tomatoes
1 cup chopped tomato
1 cup diced unpeeled cucumber
1 cup chopped onion
2 garlic cloves, minced
One 46-ounce can chilled tomato
   juice

3 tablespoons olive oil
3 tablespoons fresh lime juice
5 tablespoons red wine vinegar
1/4 to 1/2 teaspoon Tabasco sauce
1/2 teaspoon salt
1/4 teaspoon pepper

Mix all of the above ingredients together in a nonaluminum container. Cover and store in the refrigerator for several hours, or until fully chilled.

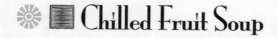 Chilled Fruit Soup

Serves 6 to 8

This soup is great on a hot summer day. It is also very quick to make.

1/2 large or 1 small watermelon
1 cantaloupe
2 cups fresh or thawed frozen unsweetened strawberries or blueberries

2 cups fresh peaches or nectarines,
   pitted, and chopped
2 to 4 cups fruit juice (we use apple-
   strawberry, but any kind you like
   will do)

Carefully remove the seeds from the watermelon, scoop out the flesh, and place it in a blender or food processor. Remove the seeds from the cantaloupe, peel, and cut into 1-inch pieces. Add the cantaloupe, strawberries or blueberries, and peaches or nectarines to the blender and blend until smooth. Add 2 cups fruit juice and blend. Add additional juice until the soup is the desired consistency; it should not be watery. Refrigerate for 1 to 2 hours, or until chilled. If served immediately, add a few ice cubes.

Salads, Sauces, and Spreads

✳ ▦ Vinaigrette Dressing

Makes 4¹/₂ cups

The egg in this dressing is optional; it helps the keep the dressing emulsified.

1 egg (optional)
1 tablespoon Dijon mustard
2 to 3 teaspoons salt
¹/₂ teaspoon pepper

1 cup white cider vinegar
2 cups canola or other mild vegetable
 oil

Whisk the eggs, mustard, salt, pepper, and vinegar in a medium bowl. Gradually whisk in the oil until the mixture is emulsified. Use as a dressing for salads or as a marinade for vegetables.

✳ ▦ Tomato–Basil Dressing

Makes 4 cups

2 tomatoes, chopped
2 tablespoons fresh basil, minced, or
 1¹/₂ teaspoons dried basil
2 garlic cloves, minced
2 teaspoons salt

2 teaspoons black pepper
1 cup red wine vinegar
1¹/₂ cups canola or other mild vegetable oil

25

In a blender or food processor, blend the tomatoes, basil, garlic, salt, pepper, and vinegar together. Add the oil as you continue to blend. Cover and store in the refrigerator for up to 2 weeks.

❋ ▦ Marinated–Mushroom Salad

Serves 4

1 pound mushrooms, whole
1¹/₂ cups Vinaigrette Dressing
 (page 25)
1 bunch green onions, sliced

¹/₂ bunch parsley, stemmed and
 minced
One 4-ounce can pimientos, chopped

Combine the mushrooms and vinaigrette, cover, and marinate for 4 to 8 hours, refrigerated. Add the remaining ingredients. Drain off most of the vinaigrette and serve.

▦ Carrot–Broccoli Salad

Serves 6

Garlic Mayonnaise
1 egg
¹/₂ teaspoon salt
¹/₄ teaspoon pepper
1 tablespoon red wine vinegar
1 ¹/₂ teaspoons Dijon mustard

1 cup canola or other mild vegetable
 oil
4 garlic cloves, minced
¹/₂ cup grated Parmesan cheese
 (optional)

❋ ❋ ❋

3 stalks broccoli, cut into bite-sized
 pieces (3 cups)
6 carrots, peeled and cut into ¹/₄-inch
 thick diagonal slices (3 cups)

Blend the egg, salt, pepper, vinegar, and mustard together in a blender or food processor. As you blend, gradually add the oil; the mixture will thicken and emulsify. Add the garlic and Parmesan cheese.

Steam the broccoli and carrots over boiling water in a covered pan until crisp-tender, about 10 minutes. Rinse under cold running water and dry them carefully on cloth or paper towels. Mix the garlic mayonnaise into the vegetables and serve.

 Pasta Salad

Serves 6

1 pound ziti pasta
One 4-ounce can pimientos, chopped
1 bunch green onions, sliced
½ bunch parsley, stemmed and
  minced

8 ounces tempeh or seitan, cubed
1 cup Vinaigrette Dressing (page 25)

Cook the pasta in a large amount of boiling water until al dente. Drain and place in a large bowl. Add the pimientos, green onions, parsley, and tempeh or seitan. Pour the vinaigrette over all and mix well.

Potato Salad

Serves 6

6 to 8 medium red, unpeeled
  potatoes, cut into 1-inch dice
  (5 cups)
2 bunches green onions, sliced
1 small bunch parsley, stemmed and
  minced (½ cup)

1 tablespoon dried dillweed
1 to 2 teaspoons salt
1 teaspoon pepper
1 cup Vinaigrette Dressing (page 25)

Place the potatoes in a large saucepan, add lightly salted water to cover, and bring to a boil. Reduce heat to a simmer and cook the potatoes until tender, about 15 minutes. Drain the potatoes, place in a bowl, and let cool. Add all the remaining ingredients. Cover and refrigerate for 1 hour.

❋ Italian Pasta Salad

Serves 6

1 pound shaped dried pasta, such as spirals, wheels, rotini, butterflies, or shells
2 tomatoes, diced
1 tablespoon minced garlic
1 cup (4 ounces) grated mozzarella or $^1/_2$ cup grated Parmesan

$^1/_2$ cup olive oil
1 tablespoon dried basil (or $^1/_2$ cup fresh, minced)
Salt to taste

Cook the pasta in a large amount of boiling salted water until al dente. Drain, place in a large bowl, and let cool. Stir in all the remaining ingredients and refrigerate for 1 to 2 hours before serving.

❋ ▦ 24-Hour Coleslaw

Serves 8

1 large head cabbage, sliced fine
6 green onions, sliced, or 1 onion, chopped
1 green bell pepper, seeds and membranes removed, finely sliced
One 4-ounce can pimientos, drained and chopped (optional)

$^3/_4$ cup cider vinegar
$^1/_2$ cup honey
1 teaspoon dry mustard powder
$1^1/_2$ teaspoon salt
1 teaspoon celery seed
$^1/_2$ cup vegetable oil

Place the vegetables in a large bowl. In a medium saucepan, bring the vinegar, honey, mustard, salt, and celery seed to a boil, then set aside and let cool. Add the oil. Pour over the vegetables, cover, and refrigerate for 24 hours, tossing several times.

 # Guacamole

Makes about 2 cups

2 ripe avocados, halved and pitted
2 tomatoes, diced
1 jalapeño chile, minced, or 1 small
    can green chilies, minced

1 bunch green onions, chopped
1/4 cup fresh lemon juice
Salt to taste

Squeeze or scoop the avocado flesh from the skin and mash it with a fork in a medium bowl. Add the tomatoes, jalapeño or green chilies (use green chilies if you want it to be less spicy), green onions, and lemon juice and mix well. Add salt.

If you are not using the guacamole immediately, cover it with a piece of plastic wrap that is pressed directly onto the surface of the guacamole to keep it from coming in contact with air, which will cause the avocado to turn brown.

 # Salsa

Makes about 5 cups

1 medium onion, chopped (1 cup)
2 garlic cloves
1 small jalapeño
1 tablespoon minced fresh cilantro
1 1/2 teaspoons red wine vinegar
2 tablespoons fresh lemon juice

2 teaspoons Tabasco sauce
1/2 teaspoon salt
Pinch of cayenne pepper
One 28-ounce can diced or whole
    tomatoes

Finely chop the onions, garlic, and jalapeño and mix them together. Add the cilantro, vinegar, lemon juice, Tabasco, salt, cayenne, and the juice from the tomatoes. Blend the tomatoes briefly to make a coarse purée and combine with the vegetables in a bowl.

✳ ▦ Middle Eastern Tofu Spread

Makes 2 cups

This is a quick alternative to traditional humus made with chickpeas, which take a long time to cook and have been known to burn up many a blender when being made into humus.

1 pound firm tofu, mashed
1/2 cup tahini (sesame paste)
5 garlic cloves, minced
1/2 cup fresh lemon juice

1/4 cup minced fresh parsley
Pinch of cayenne pepper
Salt to taste

Mash the tofu well in a bowl or blend in a blender. Add the remaining ingredients and mix well.

✳ ▦ Curry Sauce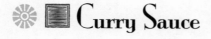

Makes 2 cups

This sauce goes well with steamed or stir-fried vegetables and rice.

1 cup yellow split peas
3 cups water
1 medium onion, chopped
   (1 1/2 cups)

4 teaspoons minced garlic
4 teaspoons minced fresh ginger root
1 1/2 teaspoons dry mustard
1 teaspoon ground cumin

$^3/_4$ teaspoon ground turmeric

$^1/_2$ teaspoon ground coriander

$^1/_2$ teaspoon ground cardamom

$^3/_4$ teaspoon black pepper

$^1/_2$ to $^3/_4$ teaspoon cayenne pepper

$1^1/_2$ teaspoons salt

Pinch of ground cinnamon

Pinch of ground cloves

$^1/_4$ cup apple juice or cider

$^1/_4$ cup dry white wine

Place the yellow split peas in a medium saucepan and add the water. Bring water to a boil and reduce to a simmer. Cook, covered, for about 1 hour until peas are soft. Heat the oil in a medium sauté pan or skillet over medium heat and sauté the onions until tender, about 10 minutes. Add garlic, ginger, and spices. In a blender or food processor, puree the cooked peas, sautéed onions, garlic, and ginger. Return the purée to the saucepan and stir in the cider and wine. Heat over low heat for 5 to 10 minutes.

 # Barbecue Sauce

Makes 3 cups

We use our barbecue sauce on seitan or tempeh served with sautéed peppers and wine and onions. Use it wherever you want a barbecue flavor.

2 cups tomato sauce

1 teaspoon smoke flavoring, if available

1 tablespoon tamari sauce or soy sauce

$^1/_4$ cup dry white wine

2 tablespoons cider vinegar

$^1/_4$ cup maple syrup

2 teaspoons dried sage

1 tablespoon black pepper

2 teaspoons dried thyme

1 tablespoon ground cumin

$^1/_2$ teaspoon cayenne pepper

1 teaspoon dried oregano

Mix all the ingredients together. Cover and refrigerate for up to 2 weeks.

 # Ketchup

Makes 4 cups

We have tried many different ketchups in the cafe over the years, but none of them were as popular with customers as standard commercial brands, which we reluctantly served. Finally, with the inspiration of our friend Elden, we decided to make our own. Our customers love it, so we no longer offer commercial ketchup. This ketchup is inexpensive to make and you will never have to wonder what the "natural flavorings" are that you find in the ingredients of commercial ketchup.

One 28-ounce can crushed tomatoes
$1/2$ cup cider vinegar
$2^1/2$ teaspoons salt
$1/2$ teaspoon black pepper
$1/2$ teaspoon dry mustard

$1/2$ teaspoon minced garlic
$1/2$ teaspoon ground cumin
2 tablespoons honey
Pinch of nutmeg

Mix all the ingredients together. Cover and refrigerate for up to 2 weeks.

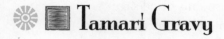 # Tamari Gravy

Makes 1 cup

$1/4$ cup canola or other mild vegetable oil
$1/4$ cup whole-wheat pastry or un-bleached all-purpose flour
$1/2$ to 1 cup water (use potato cooking water if you are making mashed potatoes to serve with the gravy)

3 tablespoons tamari sauce or soy sauce

Heat the oil in a small sauté pan or skillet over medium heat. Stir in the flour until it bubbles. Cook and stir the mixture for 1 minute. Gradually stir in the water until the gravy is the desired thickness. Add the tamari or soy sauce, stir and serve.

Main Courses

OUR CAFE IS SMALL and our kitchen staff is limited, so we prefer entrees that are not labor-intensive to prepare. This means that most of the recipes in this book are fairly simple. We only use wholesome, natural foods, but we also try to use only easily available ingredients.

 ## Vegetable Stew

Serves 6

4 cups water
1 pound firm tofu cut into ¹/₂-inch squares
4 large boiling potatoes, cut into ¹/₂-inch dice (washed well but not peeled)
4 onions, coarsely chopped

3 celery stalks cut into ¹/₂-inch pieces
2 carrots, peeled, halved lengthwise, and cut into ¹/₂-inch-thick slices
³/₄ to 1 cup tamari sauce or soy sauce
1 cup unbleached all-purpose flour
One 12-ounce package frozen peas, thawed

Tofu tends to break apart when cooked. For more durable tofu, freeze it first, then thaw. The consistency will be considerably chewier. Bring the water to a boil in a large saucepan. Add the potatoes, onions, celery, carrots, and tofu. Add the tamari or soy sauce and simmer for 30 minutes, or until tender. When the vegetables are almost done, place the flour in a small bowl and add 1 cup of the hot broth to it. Stir to make a smooth, thick paste. Add 1 cup more broth, blend, and pour into the stew. Add the peas and cook for about 5 minutes, or until the peas are tender and the stew has thickened.

❋ ▦ Stir-Fried Vegetables with Garlic-Ginger Sauce

Serves 6

Garlic-Ginger Sauce

1/4 cup minced fresh ginger
3 tablespoons minced garlic
1/2 cup finely chopped onion
1/2 cup tamari sauce or soy sauce

2 tablespoons fresh lemon juice
2 tablespoons honey
3 tablespoons dry white wine
3 tablespoons sesame or other oil

❋ ❋ ❋

4 cups water
2 cups brown rice
3 tablespoons sesame or other oil
1 cup sliced onion
1 cup sliced or matchstick-cut peeled or washed carrots
1/2 cup celery, diagonally sliced
One 8-ounce package tempeh, cut into cubes or matchsticks; or 1 pound tofu cut into 1/2-inch dice

1 cup chopped broccoli
1 small red or green bell pepper, seeds and membranes removed, chopped
1 cup sliced mushrooms
1 cup snow peas
1 cup packed stemmed greens (spinach, kale, beet greens, or other)
1 cup mung bean or other bean or grain sprouts

To make the sauce: Place all of the ingredients in a blender or food processor and blend to a smooth paste. Set aside.

Bring the water to a boil in a large saucepan over high heat. Stir in the rice.

When the water comes to a boil again, reduce heat to a simmer, cover, and cook for about 45 minutes, or until rice is tender and all the water is absorbed. Set aside and keep warm.

Heat the oil in a wok or a large skillet over high heat. Add the onion, carrot, celery, tempeh or tofu, and broccoli. Cook and stir for 2 minutes, then add the bell peppers and mushrooms. Cook and stir another 2 minutes, then add the snow peas and sprouts. Stir vegetables frequently while they are cooking to prevent burning. Add the sauce and cook for 5 minutes, or until the sauce is hot. Serve over the warm rice.

❋ ▣ Marinated-Vegetable Brochettes

Makes 8 brochettes
(serves 4)

We first created these at home in desperation to barbecue something on our outdoor grill. We hadn't discovered seitan or tempeh yet, and tofu usually fell through the grill. These worked perfectly.

Marinade

½ cup canola or other mild vegetable oil

¼ cup honey

2 tablespoons cider vinegar

2 tablespoons tamari sauce or soy sauce

2 garlic cloves, minced

2 tablespoons minced fresh parsley

1 teaspoon minced fresh ginger

1 teaspoon salt

½ teaspoon pepper

❋ ❋ ❋

1 large green or red bell pepper, seeds and membranes removed, cut into 8 wedges, each wedge halved crosswise

8 small white onions, or 1 large onion cut into eighths

8 cherry tomatoes

8 cauliflower or broccoli florets

8 large garlic cloves

1 zucchini, cut lengthwise and then into 8 thick slices (giving 16 total)

8 large white mushrooms

1 pound seitan cut into sixteen 1-ounce cubes

1½ cups brown rice (4 cups cooked)

To make the marinade: Mix all of the marinade ingredients together in a large glass baking dish. Add the vegetables and seitan to the marinade and marinate at room temperature for 2 hours, or cover and refrigerate for up to 24 hours.

Bring 3 cups of water to boil over high heat. Add the brown rice. When the water comes to a boil again, reduce heat to a simmer, cover, and cook for 45 minutes, or until rice is tender and all the water is absorbed. While rice is cooking, thread vegetables and seitan onto skewers.

If using a charcoal grill, light the charcoal. If using an oven, preheat it to 400°F, or preheat the broiler 10 minutes before cooking. To grill, place the brochettes over hot coals, brushing them frequently with marinade and turning them to prevent burning. They are done when the tomato skins begin to split open. To bake or broil, place the brochettes on a baking sheet, brush with marinade, and cook until the tomatoes begin to split, 5 to 10 minutes. Serve over rice and drizzle any remaining marinade over brochette and rice before serving.

✸ Stuffed Bell Peppers with Cheddar Cheese Sauce

Serves 4

4 green bell peppers, halved lengthwise, seeds and membranes removed
3 tablespoons olive oil
1 large onion, finely diced (2 cups)
5 garlic cloves, minced
1 teaspoon dried marjoram

$^3/_4$ cup (3 ounces) chopped walnuts
2 tomatoes, chopped
1 cup brown rice (2 cups cooked)
$^1/_4$ cup minced fresh parsley
$1^1/_2$ to 2 teaspoons salt
$^1/_2$ teaspoon pepper
2 cups water

✷ ✷ ✷

Sauce
4 tablespoons butter
$^1/_4$ cup unbleached all-purpose flour

1 cup milk
$^3/_4$ to 1 cup grated Cheddar cheese

Bring 2 cups of water to a boil in a saucepan over high heat. Add 1 cup brown rice. When the water returns to a boil, reduce heat to a simmer, cover, and cook for 45 minutes, or until rice is tender and all the water is absorbed.

Preheat the oven to 400°F. Chop one of the green peppers and set the other 4 aside. Heat the olive oil in a large sauté pan or skillet over medium heat and sauté the onions, garlic, and green pepper until tender, about 10 minutes. Add the marjoram, walnuts, and chopped tomatoes and simmer briefly. Add the rice, parsley, salt, and pepper and cook for 10 minutes. Fill the halved peppers with the rice mixture and place in a baking pan. Add a little water to the bottom of the pan and cover. Bake for 30 minutes, or until the peppers are tender.

While peppers are cooking, make the cheese sauce: Melt the butter in a medium saucepan over low heat. Stir in the flour until the mixture bubbles. Gradually stir in the milk and cook, stirring constantly, for 5 minutes, or until thickened. If the sauce is too thick, add more milk. Don't let the sauce boil. Stir in the grated cheese until it is melted. Set aside and keep warm. Place 1 stuffed pepper (two halves) on each plate, cover with warm sauce, and serve.

Eggplant Parmesan

Serves 6

2 cups unbleached all-purpose flour

5 eggs, beaten with 1 tablespoon
   water

2 cups dried whole-wheat bread
   crumbs

$1/4$ cup sesame seeds

2 tablespoons basil

1 tablespoon oregano

2 teaspoons black pepper

2 large or 4 small eggplants, cut into
   $1/4$-inch-thick slices

3 cups (12 ounces) grated mozzarella
   cheese

One 16-ounce container of ricotta
   cheese

$1/2$ cup (2 ounces) grated Parmesan
   cheese

Marinara Sauce (page 58)

Preheat the oven to 350°F. In separate bowls, place the flour in one bowl, the beaten eggs in another, and bread crumbs with the sesame seeds, basil, oregano, and black pepper in a third. Dip each slice of eggplant first in the flour, then in the eggs, and finally in the bread-crumb mixture. Place the slices on a lightly oiled baking sheet and bake until crisp on the outside and tender on the inside, about 10 to 15 minutes. Leave the oven on.

Lightly oil a 9-by-13-inch glass baking dish. Place a layer of baked eggplant slices in the pan, fitting the slices as close together as possible. Spread half of the marinara sauce on the eggplant, then the ricotta, and then sprinkle on half of the mozzarella and half of the Parmesan cheese. Repeat the layers with the remaining eggplant, sauce, and cheeses. Cover the pan with aluminum foil and bake for 20 minutes. Remove the cover and bake for 15 more minutes, or until the cheese begins to brown. Let sit at room temperature for 10 minutes before serving.

✺ Hornikopita

Serves 6

This recipe is similar to the traditional Greek dish, spanikopita, but is made without the eggs and with a mixture of vegetables rather than just with spinach. Since it's not spanikopita anymore, we've renamed it after ourselves.

1 pound fresh spinach, stemmed, or one 10-ounce package frozen spinach, thawed
3 tablespoons olive oil
2 large onions, finely chopped (4 cups)
1 pound firm tofu, mashed
3 cups finely crumbled feta cheese
6 to 8 garlic cloves, minced

2 broccoli stalks, chopped in $1/4$-inch pieces
1 pound mushrooms, sliced
2 teaspoons dried basil
2 teaspoons dried oregano
$1/2$ teaspoon each salt and pepper
1 box frozen filo dough, thawed
$1/2$ cup olive oil

Preheat the oven to 375°F. If you are using fresh spinach, steam it briefly over boiling water in a covered pan until it is wilted. Squeeze out any excess moisture. If using frozen spinach, squeeze out the excess moisture before using. Heat 3 tablespoons of the oil in a large sauté pan or skillet over medium heat and sauté the onions, garlic, broccoli, mushrooms, basil, oregano, salt, and pepper until the onions are translucent, about 10 minutes. Drain off the excess liquid, place the mixture in a large bowl, and stir in the crumbled tofu and feta.

Place 1 filo sheet in a lightly oiled 9-by-13-inch baking pan, allowing the excess filo to hang over the edge of the pan. Brush the filo with some of the $1/2$ cup of olive oil. Continue to place filo sheets in the baking pan, allowing the excess dough to hang over all the way around the pan and brushing each sheet with olive oil. Use half of the box of filo dough for this bottom layer, about 10 sheets. Place the cheese and vegetable mixture in the pan. Fold the over-hanging filo dough onto the filling. Place 1 sheet of the remaining filo on top of the filling, pushing the edges down the sides of the pan. Brush the filo with oil and repeat until all of the filo is used.

Cut several slices in the top to allow steam to escape. Bake for 30 minutes, or until the filo is golden brown. Let sit for 10 minutes before serving. Cut into 3- or 4-inch squares.

❋ ▦ ▤ Tofu–Vegetable Quiche

Serves 6

This recipe was given to us by Vivian, one of our regular customers. It is an egg-free version of quiche, filled with garlicky tofu, nuts, and a colorful assortment of vegetables.

$3/4$ cup (3 ounces) raw cashews

1 pound firm tofu, mashed

2 tablespoons arrowroot or cornstarch

3 tablespoons olive oil, plus olive oil for brushing

1 large onion, chopped (2 cups)

6 to 8 garlic cloves, minced

2 celery stalks, chopped

1 green bell pepper, seeds and membranes removed, diced

1 red bell pepper, seeds and membranes removed, diced

$1^1/2$ cups (5 ounces) mushrooms, sliced

2 stalks broccoli, chopped (2 cups)

2 teaspoons dried basil

1 teaspoon salt

1 teaspoon pepper

One 10-inch pie crust (page 99)

Preheat the oven to 350°F. Chop the cashews very fine in a blender or food processor. Add the tofu and arrowroot or cornstarch to the cashews and blend well. Heat the 3 tablespoons oil in a sauté pan or skillet over medium heat and sauté the onions, garlic, celery, bell peppers, mushrooms, broccoli, basil, salt, and pepper until tender, about 10 minutes. Add the tofu mixture to the vegetables and mix well. Place in the pie shell. Brush the top with a little olive oil to prevent drying and bake for 35 minutes, or until brown.

❋ ▦ West African Stew

Serves 6 to 8

2 pounds sweet potatoes, peeled and cut into ½-inch dice (about 4 cups)

¼ cup olive oil

2 tablespoons minced garlic

2 tablespoons minced fresh ginger

2 to 3 large onions, chopped (5 cups)

2 to 3 eggplants, peeled and cut into 1-inch dice (6 cups)

5 to 6 fresh tomatoes, chopped, or one 28-ounce can diced tomatoes

2 large green bell peppers, seeds and membranes removed, chopped (2 cups)

2 medium zucchini and/or summer squash, cut into half-moon slices (2 cups)

1 cup peanut butter

2 tablespoons plus 1 teaspoon ground coriander

½ to 1 teaspoon cayenne pepper

Salt to taste

Couscous

2 cups couscous

4 cups boiling water

1 teaspoon salt

❋ ❋ ❋

Place the sweet potatoes in a saucepan and cover with water. Cook until just tender, about 10 minutes after the water begins to boil. Drain and set aside. (Save the liquid to add to the stew if it is too dry.)

Heat the oil in a large sauté pan or skillet over medium heat and sauté the garlic and ginger for 3 minutes. Add the chopped onions and cook until the onions are translucent, about 10 minutes. Add the eggplant and the fresh tomatoes, if using. Cook for 10 minutes, stirring frequently. Add the green peppers and zucchini or squash and cook until tender, about 10 more minutes. Add the tomatoes, sweet potatoes, peanut butter, coriander, cayenne, and salt, and mix well. Set aside and keep warm.

To make the couscous: In a medium saucepan, add the salt to the water and bring to a boil. Add the couscous. Cover and let sit for 5 minutes or until all the water is absorbed. Fluff with a fork. Serve the warm stew over the couscous.

▣ Egg Rolls with Sweet–and–Sour Orange Sauce

Makes approximately 20

Egg rolls not only make a delicious meal, they also make a great appetizer.

Egg Roll Filling

3 tablespoons canola or other mild vegetable oil

6 to 8 large cloves garlic, minced

1½ to 2 walnut-sized pieces fresh ginger, minced

1 bunch green onions, chopped

2 carrots, chopped (about 1 cup)

1 bunch parsley, chopped

4 stalks celery, chopped (about 1 cup)

1 pound firm tofu, cut into ¼-inch dice

1 cup mushrooms, sliced

6 to 8 tablespoons tamari sauce

1 8-ounce package bean sprouts

1 package egg roll wrappers

Canola oil or other mild vegetable oil for frying egg rolls

✳   ✳   ✳

Sweet-and-Sour Orange Sauce

4 cloves garlic, minced

$^1/_2$ walnut-sized piece of fresh ginger minced

$^3/_4$ cup orange juice

1 tablespoon orange peel, minced

4 tablespoons tamari sauce

4 tablespoons cider vinegar

4 tablespoons honey

1 tablespoon prepared mustard or 1$^1/_2$ teaspoons dry mustard

1 tablespoon arrowroot or corn starch

To make the filling: Heat 3 tablespoons oil in a cast iron pan or other large pan. Add garlic, ginger, green onions, carrots, parsley, celery, tofu, and mushrooms, and cook for about 10 minutes until all vegetables are hot. Add bean sprouts and remove from heat and let cool enough to handle comfortably.

To make the egg rolls: Take one egg roll wrapper and place it on flat surface in front of you with one corner pointing directly towards you. Place about $^1/_3$ cup of filling in the middle of the wrapper, just below the center. Fold the bottom corner over the filling until the corner point touches the dough above the mound of filling. Fold the right and left corners over the filling until they touch each other. Moisten the remaining unfolded corner with water so it will stick to the rest of the roll. Finish the egg roll by rolling it away from you, toward the remaining unfolded corner. Roll up the remaining egg rolls and set them aside. (Do not stack them on top of each other, or they may all stick together.)

To make the sauce: Combine garlic, ginger, orange juice, orange peel, tamari, vinegar, honey, mustard, and arrowroot or corn starch in a blender and mix well. Pour into a sauce pan and cook over medium heat until sauce thickens. Remove from heat.

Cook egg rolls in about $^1/_4$ inch of vegetable oil heated to 375° F, turning until all sides are browned. When rolls are done cooking, remove from oil and place on paper towels to dry. (Alternatively, you can bake the egg rolls on a lightly oiled baking sheet for 20 minutes at 350° F.) Serve with Sweet-and-Sour Orange Sauce for dipping.

❋ ▦ Holiday Tofu Turkey

Serves 4

My wife and I invented this dish years ago to serve for special occasions. We usually serve it on Thanksgiving with mashed potatoes and gravy, cranberry sauce, peas, and dinner rolls, with pumpkin pie for dessert. This recipe takes some advance work, so plan several days ahead before you intend to serve it.

32 ounces firm tofu
2 tablespoons tamari sauce or soy
    sauce
1 tablespoon dry sherry
1 tablespoon hot sesame oil or
    1 tablespoon vegetable oil with
    $1/2$ teaspoon dried red pepper flakes
    added
2 tablespoons water
$1/2$ teaspoon pepper

Several days before you are planning to serve this meal, freeze the tofu. If you buy tofu prepackaged in 1 pound blocks, just place two of these in your freezer overnight. If you buy your tofu in bulk, tightly pack 32 ounces of tofu (4 squares, usually) in a container, cover with water, seal and freeze overnight. The freezing process changes the texture of the tofu, giving it a chewy consistency. The day before cooking the tofu, remove it from the freezer and let it thaw at room temperature for about 6 to 8 hours. Squeeze excess water out of tofu by pressing down on it with your hand. Place the thawed tofu in a glass loaf pan or other oven-safe pan.

In a small bowl, mix the tamari or soy sauce, sherry, oil, and water together. Pour this marinade over the tofu, cover, and marinate overnight. The next day, preheat the oven to 350°F. Sprinkle the tofu with some pepper, baste it with the marinade, and bake for 1½ hours, basting the tofu periodically with the marinade as it cooks.

Mexican Dishes

While some of our Mexican creations are made with ingredients that won't be found on your next trip to Mexico, you won't mistake the taste of the finished product. If you like hot and spicy Mexican food, these recipes will be fine. If you like milder food, cut back on the amount of the chilies called for. You can always add cayenne pepper or dried pepper flakes to spice it up if you find that a dish is too mild.

 ## Refried Beans

Makes 7 to 8 cups

Although it is not a main dish, refried beans is included here because it is the basis of so many Mexican dishes.

3 cups dried pinto beans
1 to 2 garlic cloves, minced
1 jalapeño chili, minced, or
    1 teaspoon red chili pepper flakes
2 tablespoons chili powder
2 tablespoons ground cumin

¼ teaspoon ground coriander
1 teaspoon salt
¼ cup nutritional yeast

Carefully pick through the pinto beans to remove any rocks or other foreign matter. Rinse the beans well, place them in a large pot, and add water to cover them by several inches. Cover the pot loosely and bring to a boil. Lower heat to a simmer and cook, covered, for $2^1/_2$ to 3 hours, or until the beans are tender. Stir beans occasionally while they cook and add additional water, if needed. To test for doneness, squeeze a bean between your fingers. It will offer little resistance if it is done.

To reduce the cooking time of the beans, place the rinsed beans in the pressure cooker with 4 times their volume of water and cook at 15 pounds pressure (the amount of water will vary depending upon how much steam your pressure cooker releases during cooking). Check the beans for doneness after 1 hour. Alternatively, soak the beans for 3 to 4 hours, or overnight; this will reduce the cooking time by 30 minutes to 1 hour.

Add the garlic, jalapeños, spices, salt, and the nutritional yeast to the cooked beans. Mash them with a potato masher until they are somewhat smooth.

Bean, Cheese, and Vegetable Burrito
Spread 1 large spoonful of refried beans down the center of a flour tortilla. On top of this, add any, or all, of the following: grated Cheddar cheese, diced tomatoes, chopped green onions, chopped black olives, chopped lettuce or sprouts, avocado or guacamole, sour cream, and salsa. Roll up and enjoy!

Tostadas
Crisp corn tortillas on a baking sheet in the oven for a few minutes at 400°F. Spread refried beans over each tortilla and top with any of the items listed for burritos.

 # Nachos

*Makes an appetizer for
6 to 8 people*

This makes a good snack or appetizer for a Mexican dinner and is easy to make.

One 16-ounce bag tortilla chips
3 cups refried beans (page 48)
3 cups (1 pound) grated Cheddar or
mozzarella cheese, or both

$^{1}/_{2}$ to 2 teaspoons dried red pepper
flakes (optional)
Salsa (page 29)

Preheat the oven to 350°F. Place a layer several chips thick on an oven-proof plate. Spread or drop spoonfuls of refried beans over the tortilla chips. (If the refried beans are very thick, thin them with a little water so they may be more easily spread over the chips.) Sprinkle grated cheese over the beans. Sprinkle with red pepper flakes, if you like. Top with a thin layer of chips and sprinkle more grated cheese on top. Bake for 5 minutes, or until cheese is melted. Serve with the salsa.

 # Spicy Black Beans

Makes 8 cups

These beans may be used in burritos, tostadas, or in any other dish using refried beans. An especially good and easy combination is black beans and brown rice.

3 cups dried black beans
6 cups water
3 tablespoons canola or other mild
vegetable oil
1 onion, chopped (about $1^{1}/_{2}$ cups)
1 green bell pepper, seeds and membranes removed, chopped

3 to 4 garlic cloves, minced
1 jalapeño chili pepper, minced
2 teaspoon salt
1 tablespoon dried basil
$1^{1}/_{2}$ teaspoons ground cumin
$^{1}/_{4}$ to $^{1}/_{2}$ teaspoon cayenne pepper

Sort through the black beans to remove any rocks or other foreign matter. Rinse the beans. Black beans cook more quickly than many other beans, so they don't require soaking. Place the beans and water in a large pot and bring to a boil. Reduce heat to a simmer and cook, covered, for $1^{1}/_{2}$ to 2 hours. Check the beans frequently and add water to cover as necessary. When the beans are tender, remove them from heat. Drain off any excess water covering beans, but save it to add back in if beans are too dry.

While the beans are cooking, heat the oil in a medium sauté pan or skillet over medium heat. Add the onion, green pepper, garlic, and jalapeño and sauté until tender, about 10 minutes. Add the salt, basil, cumin, and cayenne and stir the mixture into the beans. Cook 10 minutes more on low heat to allow flavors to blend.

✳ Enchiladas Nuevo Leone

Makes 8 large enchiladas

The unusual filling for these mildly spicy enchiladas contains potatoes, beans, onion, pickles, and cheese. We often have to convince customers to try it, but they are rarely dissatisfied.

Filling

1 1/2 pounds potatoes, peeled and cut into 1/4-inch dice (5 cups)

3 tablespoons canola or other mild vegetable oil

2 medium onions, finely chopped (2 cups)

5 garlic cloves, minced

1 tablespoon ground cumin

1 1/2 teaspoon ground coriander

1 teaspoon salt

1 teaspoon pepper

2 cups refried beans (see page 48)

Dill pickles, finely chopped (1 1/2 cups)

1 cup fresh or thawed frozen corn kernels

3/4 cup (3 ounces) grated Cheddar cheese, plus 1/2 cup Cheddar cheese for topping (optional)

❋ ❋ ❋

Sauce

One 16-ounce can tomato sauce

1 tablespoon chili powder

1 tablespoon minced garlic

❋ ❋ ❋

Eight 8-inch flour tortillas (page 75)

Preheat the oven to 350°F. *To make the filling:* Cook the diced potatoes in boiling water until they are done but still firm, about 10 minutes. Heat the oil in a large sauté pan or skillet over medium heat and sauté the onion and garlic until translucent, about 10 minutes. Add the cumin, coriander, salt, and pepper and cook a few minutes more. Stir in the beans, pickles, corn, potatoes, and cheese, and set aside.

To make the sauce, combine all of the ingredients in a medium bowl. Spread a thin layer of sauce on one side of a flour tortilla. Spoon 1 to 1½ cups of the filling down the center of each tortilla. Roll the tortilla around the filling and place it in a lightly oiled 9-by-13-inch baking dish, seam side down. Repeat with the rest of the tortillas and filling. Spread the remaining sauce over the top of the enchiladas. Top them with additional grated cheese, if desired. Cover the dish and bake for 45 minutes to 1 hour.

✳ Vegetable Cheese Enchiladas

Serves 6

Every Wednesday, we serve a Mexican special at the cafe. Some days you feel like trying something different. Here is a recipe that we created which is very popular. It is now a frequent special.

1 small carrot, peeled or washed well

1 small zucchini

2 tablespoons canola or other mild vegetable oil

4 garlic cloves, chopped

2 medium onions, cut into thin, 1-inch strips

2 green bell peppers, seeds and membranes removed, cut into 1-inch-long strips

2 jalapeño chilies, minced

½ teaspoon ground coriander

1 tablespoon ground cumin

½ teaspoon dried red pepper flakes

12 corn tortillas (page 76)

2 cups (8 ounces) grated Cheddar cheese

Salsa and sour cream for serving

Preheat the oven to 350°F. Cut the carrot in half lengthwise and slice into thin half-moons. Quarter the zucchini and cut into ¼-inch slices.

Heat the oil in a large skillet or wok over medium-high heat. Add the garlic, onions, peppers, and carrots, and sauté until the onions are golden, about 10 minutes. Add the zucchini, coriander, cumin, and pepper flakes, and cook until the zucchini is tender, about 3 minutes more.

In order to roll the filling inside the corn tortillas, the tortillas must be soft. If you are using fresh tortillas, you should have no problem. If using frozen tortillas, soften them first by frying for several seconds in a little oil or salsa.

Place a line of grated cheese down the center of a soft tortilla. Spread a large spoonful of vegetables over the cheese. Fold the edge of the tortilla nearest you over the vegetables and roll the tortilla. Place the filled tortilla seam side down in a lightly oiled baking pan. Repeat to use all the tortillas and filling. Sprinkle the remaining cheese over the top and bake for 10 to 15 minutes, or until cheese is melted. Serve with salsa and sour cream.

NOTE: If you have any cooked rice handy, place a 1-inch layer on the bottom of the baking pan with a little water (¼ cup) before you add the enchiladas. The rice will heat up along with the enchiladas and give you a ready side dish.

✳ Seitan Fajitas

Serves 6 to 8

2 tablespoons canola or other mild vegetable oil

3 green bell peppers, seeds and membranes removed, cut into thin 1-inch strips (3 cups)

2 medium onions, cut into thin strips

3 garlic cloves, minced

2 jalapeño chilies, minced

1 pound seitan, cut into strips ¼-inch thick and 1-inch long

2 cups fresh or thawed frozen corn kernels

2 teaspoons ground cumin

½ teaspoon ground coriander

dash of salt, or to taste

2 cups (8 ounces) grated Cheddar cheese (optional)

6 to 8 flour tortillas (page 76)

Preheat the oven to 350°F. Heat the oil in a skillet or wok over medium heat. Add the onions, peppers, garlic, and jalapeños and sauté until tender, about 10 minutes. Add the seitan, corn, cumin, coriander, and salt to the vegetables and sauté for about 5 minutes, until thoroughly heated.

Place a line of cheese (optional) down the center of a tortilla. Spoon ³/₄ cup of the seitan filling onto the tortilla. Fold the tortilla edge closest to you over filling and roll so that the seam side is down. Place the rolled fajitas in a lightly oiled baking pan and top with the remaining cheese. Bake for 10 to 15 minutes, or until the cheese is melted.

✳ Broccoli–Sour Cream Enchiladas

Serves 6

5 stalks broccoli, chopped (5 cups)
3 tablespoons olive oil or canola oil
2 medium onions, finely chopped
    (2 cups)
2 jalapeño chilies, minced
4 garlic cloves, minced
1 teaspoon salt
2 teaspoons ground cumin

¹/₂ teaspoon ground coriander
¹/₄ to ¹/₂ teaspoon cayenne pepper
    (optional)
1 cup sour cream
2 cups (8 ounces) grated Cheddar
    cheese
12 corn tortillas (page 76)

Steam the broccoli over boiling water in a covered pot for 10 minutes, or until tender. Heat the oil in a large sauté pan or skillet over medium heat and cook the onions, garlic, jalapeños, salt, cumin, coriander, and cayenne, if using, for 10 minutes, or until tender. Remove from heat and add the sour cream, broccoli, and 1 cup of the grated cheese.

Corn tortillas must be soft for rolling up. If they are at all brittle, fry them for several seconds in a little oil or salsa just until soft. Place a line of ¹/₄ cup filling down the center of a tortilla. Fold the tortilla edge closest to you over the top of the filling and roll it up. Repeat with the remaining tortillas and filling. Place the enchiladas seam side down in an oiled baking dish. Top with the remaining 1 cup grated cheese. Bake for 10 to 15 minutes, or until cheese is melted.

Pasta Dishes

We have several pasta dishes on our menu and feature pasta specials often. Pasta is very nutritious and, with a vegetable sauce and a tossed salad, makes a complete meal. Most pasta dishes call for cheese of some sort, but we have included several non-dairy recipes for those wishing to limit their dairy intake.

Cooking Pasta

Use plenty of boiling water—about 4 quarts for 1 pound of pasta. One pound of pasta will make 4 generous servings. When the water is boiling hard, add 4 teaspoons salt. Let the water come to a boil again, then add the pasta. Stir the pasta now and several more times while it is cooking to prevent the pasta from sticking together or to the bottom of the pot. Once the pot has returned to a boil, fresh pasta may cook in 2 to 4 minutes, dried pasta in 8 to 12 minutes, depending on the pasta. Test a piece frequently to see if it is done. Perfectly cooked pasta is al dente, or still slightly firm in the center. Drain the pasta and toss with a little oil to prevent it from sticking together.

✳ Roasted Red Pepper Pesto

Serves 4

Here is an alternative to the traditional fresh basil pesto that has become popular in recent years.

5 large red bell peppers
6 garlic cloves
$^{1}/_{2}$ cup (2 ounces) pine nuts or
    walnuts
$^{3}/_{4}$ cup olive oil

1 cup grated Parmesan cheese
Dash of salt and pepper
1 pound fresh or dried fettuccine or
    linguine

Place the whole peppers directly on the racks in a preheated 500°F oven for 20 to 30 minutes, turning them occasionally, until they are fully blackened. Cover the bottom of the oven with foil first, or place baking sheets below the peppers to catch any drips. Alternatively, cut the peppers in half lengthwise, remove the stems, seeds, and membranes, and place them open-side down on a broiler pan. Broil until the skins turn evenly black. Place the peppers in a bowl, cover, and let sit for 10 minutes to cool. Remove the skins from the peppers with your fingers.

    Place the peeled peppers, garlic, nuts, oil, Parmesan, salt, and pepper in a blender or food processor and blend until smooth. You should have approximately 2 cups of purée. Cook and drain the pasta according to the instructions on page 55. Mix the purée with hot pasta, tossing well, and serve.

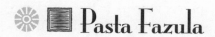 Pasta Fazula

Serves 4

I'm not sure which of our four children coined this name, but we use it for any pasta invention that we make at home. This one is easy to make, different, and tasty.

4 tablespoons olive oil
1 onion, chopped
5 to 6 garlic cloves, minced
8 ounces mushrooms, sliced
One 8-ounce package tempeh, cut
    into small cubes

1 red bell pepper, seeds and membranes removed, chopped
$^{1}/_{4}$ cup dry sherry
Salt and pepper to taste
1 pound fresh or dried pasta
1 cup tomatoes, diced (optional)

Heat the oil in a large sauté pan or skillet over medium heat and cook the onion, garlic, mushrooms, and tempeh for about 10 minutes. Add red pepper and sherry. Cook until most of the sherry is evaporated. Add the salt and pepper.

While the sauce is cooking, cook the pasta according to the directions on page 55. Toss the pasta with the warm sauce and serve.

Pasta with Hot Garlic Sauce

Serves 4

1 cup olive oil
1 tablespoon dried red pepper flakes
   (use less for a milder dish)
12 garlic cloves, minced
$^1/_2$ teaspoon salt

$^1/_4$ cup dried basil
1 pound fresh or dried linguine or
   fettuccine
1 cup minced fresh parsley

Heat the olive oil in a medium sauté pan or skillet over medium heat. Add the pepper flakes, garlic, salt, and basil, reduce heat to low, and cook until the garlic is golden, about 4 minutes. Meanwhile, cook the pasta according to the directions on page 55. Pour the warm sauce over the drained pasta, add the parsley, toss together, and serve.

VARIATIONS
Add small cubes of tofu or mushrooms to the oil when sautéing the garlic and spices.

❈ ▦ Pasta with Marinara Sauce and Tofu Balls

Serves 4

Marinara Sauce

3 tablespoons olive oil

5 garlic cloves, minced

1/2 green bell pepper, seeds and membranes removed, finely chopped

1 onion, finely chopped

1 teaspoon dried basil

1 teaspoon dried oregano

1/4 teaspoon dried red pepper flakes

1 tablespoon honey

1/4 cup dry red wine

One 28-ounce can tomato sauce

Tofu Balls

1 pound firm tofu, well mashed

1/2 cup dried whole-wheat bread crumbs

2 tablespoons tamari sauce or soy sauce

1/4 cup finely chopped onion

4 garlic cloves, minced

1/3 cup nutritional yeast

1/2 teaspoon dried oregano

1 teaspoon dried basil

1/2 teaspoon pepper

2 eggs, beaten (optional)

* * *

1 pound fresh or dried linguine

To make the sauce: Heat the oil in a large sauté pan or skillet, cast iron if you have one, over medium heat, and cook the garlic, onion, bell peppers, basil, red pepper flakes, and oregano until the vegetables are tender, about 10 minutes. Add the honey and wine and cook until half of the liquid has evaporated. Add the tomato sauce, reduce heat to low, and cook until thick, about 1 hour. Set aside.

To make the tofu balls: Preheat the oven to 400°F. Combine all the ingredients in a large bowl and mix well. The optional eggs will make the tofu balls hold together better when they are cooked but will not improve the taste. Form the mixture into balls about 1¼ inches in diameter and place on a lightly oiled baking sheet. Bake for 30 minutes, or until browned. Cook the pasta according to the directions on page 55. Serve with warm tofu balls, topped with warm marinara sauce.

✳ Baked Pasta Casserole

Serves 6

Sauce

¼ cup olive oil
3 medium onions, finely chopped
 (3 cups)
4 garlic cloves, minced
One 28-ounce can whole tomatoes
One 6-ounce can tomato paste
2 tablespoons minced fresh parsley

1 teaspoon salt
1 tablespoon honey
1 teaspoon dried oregano
1 teaspoon dried basil
¼ teaspoon pepper

✳ ✳ ✳

Cheese Layer

32 ounces ricotta or cottage cheese
2 cups (8 ounces) shredded mozzarella cheese

⅔ cup (3 ounces) Parmesan cheese
1 tablespoon minced fresh parsley
¼ teaspoon pepper

✳ ✳ ✳

1 pound ziti pasta
3 tablespoons grated Parmesan cheese

To make the sauce: Heat oil in a large sauté pan or skillet over medium heat. Sauté the garlic and onions until golden, about 10 minutes. Add the remaining ingredients, crushing the whole tomatoes with a fork. Simmer, covered, for 1 hour, stirring occasionally. Thin the sauce, if necessary, with a little water. Set aside and keep warm.

To make the cheese layer: Mix all of the cheese layer ingredients together in a large bowl and set aside. Preheat the oven to 350°F. Cook the pasta according to the directions on page 55. Spread a small amount of the cheese mixture in the bottom of a 5-quart casserole. Top with one-third of the drained ziti, then one-third of the cheese mixture and one-third of the remaining sauce. Repeat the layers. Top with the Parmesan cheese and bake, uncovered, for 45 minutes.

Pizzas

Tuesday is pizza day at the cafe and has been for many years, even though there are probably a dozen pizza restaurants in the area. We don't try to be competitive with these other restaurants, we try to be more creative.

❋ ▣ Whole–Wheat Pizza Dough

Makes one 16-inch crust

1$\frac{1}{2}$ cups warm water (should feel warm on the inside of your wrist, not hot)

2 teaspoons (1 package) active dried yeast

1$\frac{1}{2}$ teaspoons salt

1 tablespoon honey

3 tablespoons olive oil

1$\frac{1}{2}$ teaspoons dried basil (optional)

$\frac{1}{4}$ teaspoon pepper (optional)

2 cups whole-wheat bread flour

1$\frac{1}{2}$ to 2 cups unbleached all-purpose flour

Place the warm water in a large bowl and stir in the yeast, salt, honey, olive oil, basil, and pepper. Stir in the whole-wheat flour 1 cup at a time, then stir in the unbleached all-purpose flour 1 cup at a time until the dough pulls away from the sides of the bowl.

Turn the dough out onto a lightly floured surface. If any dough remains in the bowl, add a little flour and rub the sides of the bowl until the dough falls away. Knead the dough, adding in additional flour as necessary, until the dough is smooth and springy (see page 69 for instructions on kneading). Oil a large bowl, place the dough in the bowl, and turn the dough over to coat it with oil. Cover with a cloth and let rise in a warm place to rise until double, 30 minutes to 1 hour.

Punch the dough down and form it into a ball. Place the dough on a lightly floured surface and flatten it to a 1-inch thickness, keeping the dough as round as possible. Roll the dough out with a rolling pin, turning the dough over and rotating it ½ turn each time to keep it round. Roll the dough out to a 18-inch-diameter circle.

Sprinkle a small amount of cornmeal onto a 16-inch pizza pan. Place the dough on the pan and roll up the overhanging dough to make an edge.

Basic Pizza

Preheat the oven to 425°F. Spread 2 cups marinara sauce (see page 58) over prepared crust. Add desired toppings (sliced onions, peppers, garlic, tomatoes, lightly steamed broccoli, etc.). Finish with 2 cups (½ pound) grated mozzarella cheese spread evenly over the top. Bake for 15 minutes, or until cheese is lightly browned.

 Tempeh Sausage Pizza

Makes one 16-inch pizza

The topping may not fool the sausage lover in your family, but it's a great no-cholesterol alternative for pizza (or for any other recipe using sausage).

One 8-ounce package tempeh, crumbled
1 tablespoon dried fennel seed
1 teaspoon dried basil
1 teaspoon dried oregano
1/2 teaspoon dried red pepper flakes

1/2 teaspoon rubbed or powdered sage
2 teaspoons garlic, minced
8 teaspoons tamari sauce or soy sauce
1 tablespoon canola oil
Whole Wheat Pizza Dough (page 60)

In a large bowl, combine all of the ingredients except the oil and pizza dough, pressing the herbs into the tempeh as you mix. Heat the oil in a large sauté pan or skillet over medium heat and cook the mixture until lightly browned, about 5 to 10 minutes.

Add Tempeh Sausage to any other pizza toppings and bake as directed.

Tofu Pesto Pizza

Makes one 16-inch pizza

The pesto is an excellent non dairy pizza topping when combined with marinara sauce and assorted vegetables.

3 tablespoons olive oil
3 garlic cloves
1/2 cup packed fresh basil leaves, or 3 tablespoons dried basil

2 tablespoons pine nuts or walnuts
2 tablespoons minced fresh parsley
1 teaspoon tamari sauce or soy sauce
1/4 teaspoon pepper

³/₄ teaspoon nutritional yeast

2 ounces tofu

3 cups assorted sliced fresh vegetables, such as onions, green
peppers, tomatoes, mushrooms,
steamed broccoli, spinach, garlic,
and olives

Whole-Wheat Pizza Dough (page 60)

2 cups Marinara Sauce (page 58)

Preheat the oven to 400°F. Place all the pesto ingredients in blender or food processor and blend until smooth. Spread a thin layer of tofu pesto onto the prepared pizza crust. Add a layer of vegetables and top with 2 cups marinara sauce. Bake for 15 minutes, or until crust is slightly browned.

 # Greek Pizza

Makes one 16-inch pizza

2 cups Marinara Sauce (page 58)

One recipe Whole-Wheat Pizza
Dough (page 60)

³/₄ cup sliced mushrooms

1¹/₂ cups spinach leaves, shredded or
chopped

6 garlic cloves

10 to 12 black or Greek olives, sliced
or chopped

4 to 6 ounces feta cheese, crumbled

1 cup (4 ounces) grated mozzarella
cheese

Preheat the oven to 425°F. Spread the sauce on the pizza crust. Add the mushrooms, spinach, garlic, olives, feta, and finally the mozzarella. Bake for 15 minutes, or until cheese is lightly browned.

Green Mediterranean Pizza

Makes one 16-inch pizza

This pizza was created one day by Matt, a cook at the cafe. It has turned out to be incredibly popular. The cheese mixture in the recipe also makes an excellent omelet filling.

2 cups Marinara Sauce (page 58)
Whole-Wheat Pizza Dough (page 60)
1 tomato, thinly sliced
1 tablespoon olive oil

* * *

Cheese Mixture

1/4 cup minced fresh dillweed, (1 tablespoon dried dillweed may be substituted but it is not nearly as good)
1/2 cup packed fresh spinach leaves, minced
2/3 cup onion, chopped fine
5 garlic cloves, minced
3/4 cup finely crumbled feta
1 cup (3 ounces) grated mozzarella cheese

Preheat the oven to 425°F. Spread the marinara sauce on the pizza crust. Evenly space the tomato slices on top of the sauce. *To make the cheese mixture:* Add minced dill, spinach, onions, and garlic to a medium-sized bowl. Add feta and mozzarella and mix well. Sprinkle the cheese mixture onto the pizza. Top with a drizzle of olive oil to keep the topping moist while baking. Bake for 15 minutes, or until the cheese is lightly browned.

Breads and Muffins

I AM VERY PROUD OF THE BREADS that we bake at the cafe. Not only are they flavorful, they are nutritious. We regularly bake whole-wheat and raisin breads and, occasionally, French bread. People often ask to buy loaves of our bread, but we usually don't have enough to sell. In the summer we bake two or three times a week; in winter, once or twice per week. We freeze the bread that won't be used in the next day or two to keep it fresh. We never refrigerate our bread because it makes it dry and crumbly. To freeze bread, let it cool thoroughly after baking, then place in a tightly sealed plastic bag. It will thaw in about two hours at room temperature when you want it.

Of all the things that we cook at the cafe, probably the most varied is muffins. We bake muffins every day for breakfast, and we sell them all day long. Some kinds always sell well, such as blueberry and maple-corn. Other kinds, such as brown rice muffins (one of my favorites), may sound too ordinary and we never know how well they will sell.

Most of our muffin recipes originally called for eggs, as do most muffin recipes you will find. Since some of our customers do not eat eggs, however, we began experimenting with ways to make our muffins egg-free. We finally came up with a simple substitution of 1 tablespoon of yogurt for each egg called for in the recipe. In addition, we increased the amount of liquid slightly, since the yogurt has less liquid volume than the egg it is replacing. We now make all of our muffins without eggs.

The same people who wanted egg-free muffins also asked about egg-free pancakes. I hesitated to change our pancake recipe because ours are the best pancakes around. Instead, we made up some dry pancake mix and made egg-free pancakes to order, using the same substitution of 1 tablespoon of yogurt for 1 egg, as used in our muffins. After a few weeks of doing this, and numerous taste tests among the customers and staff, we began making all of our pancakes with yogurt instead of eggs.

Breads

The sourdough French and rye bread served at the Horn of the Moon Cafe are baked by Upland Bakers, a couple in Plainfield, Vermont, who use a homemade wood-fired stone oven. Their breads are so popular that local stores limit customers' purchases to no more than two loaves at a time.

We bake our own whole-wheat and raisin breads and, on occasion, whole-wheat French bread, but since we can bake only two dozen loaves, we're not able to sell loaves of our bread. Since we bake only a few times each week, we often freeze much of our bread after it has cooled. We don't store our bread in the refrigerator, because this makes it dry and crumbly. It's a much better idea to set aside as much bread as you will eat in two or three days, then freeze the rest.

 # Whole Grain Bread

Makes two 9-by-5-inch loaves

2³/4 cups warm water (it should feel barely warm on the inside of your wrist)

4 teaspoons(2 packages) active dried yeast

5 tablespoons canola or other mild vegetable oil

5 tablespoons honey

¹/3 cup raw wheat germ

¹/2 cup rolled oats

1 tablespoon salt

1 tablespoon nutritional yeast (optional)

2$^1/_2$ cups unbleached all-purpose flour
(with germ added back, if available)
2$^1/_2$ to 3 cups whole-wheat bread flour
Oil or melted butter for brushing on
crust

Add the warm water to a large bowl. Add the dried yeast, oil, honey, wheat germ, oats, salt, and nutritional yeast, and mix with wooden spoon. Stir in the all-purpose flour 1 cup at a time, always stirring in the same direction so that you do not break the developing gluten strands that will make the bread light. When you have added all of the all-purpose flour, stir the mixture 100 times in the same direction. This helps to develop the gluten and reduces the amount of time you will have to knead the dough.

Stir in the whole-wheat flour 1 cup at a time. When the dough becomes too stiff to stir with a spoon, use your hand, continuing to mix in the same direction in which you were stirring. Keep mixing the dough and adding flour until the dough pulls away from the sides of the bowl. Turn the dough out onto a lightly floured surface. If there is still dough stuck in the bowl, add a little flour to the bowl and rub the sides of the bowl with your hand. This works to remove dough from your hands as well. Add the resulting clumps to the dough to be kneaded.

To knead the dough, press it out flat with the heels of your hands on the floured surface. If the dough feels sticky, add a little flour. After you have pressed the dough out flat, fold the top half over onto the bottom half and again press the dough out flat. Rotate the dough 90 degrees and fold the top down over the bottom half of the dough again. Continue this process for about 10 minutes, or until the dough is smooth and not sticky, and it springs slowly back to its original shape when you press your finger into it.

Oil your bread bowl and add the dough to it. Turn the dough over so the top side is coated with oil. Cover the bowl with a cloth and place it in a warm spot to rise until the dough is doubled, about 1 hour. Punch the dough down with your fist and knead a few times to get some of the air bubbles out. Cut the dough in half. With a rolling pin, roll the dough out flat to remove any remaining air bubbles. Roll the dough up in a tight roll with your hands. Using the edge of your hands, "karate chop" the dough several inches from each end and fold the dough flaps under. Using your hands, shape the dough until it is a fairly uniform log shape about the same length as the loaf pans. Oil or butter the pans and place the dough, seam side down, in the pans so that the ends of each loaf touch the ends of the pan. Let the dough rise in a warm place, uncovered, until it is doubled and rising over the top of the bread pan, about 1 hour. Don't let it rise too much or you may have large air bubbles under the crust or the loaves may collapse in the hot oven. Your loaves will continue to rise after placing them in the oven until the heat kills the yeast.

About 20 minutes before baking, preheat the oven to 375°F. Place the bread on the middle rack in the oven, and bake for 40 minutes, or until nicely browned. To check for doneness, turn a loaf out onto a table and thump the bottom of the loaf with your finger. If it has a hollow sound, it is done. If not, put it back into the pan and return it to the oven for a while longer. When done, remove the loaves from the pans. If the bread sticks, rap the bottom of the pan on a hard surface and it should slide right out. Brush oil or butter on top of the loaves while they are still hot to keep them moist. Let the loaves cool fully before putting them in plastic bags to store.

✳ Spinach-Cheese Braids

Makes 2 braids and 1 whole-grain loaf

Serve this savory bread with its filling of spinach, onions, and two kinds of cheese with a salad for lunch or a light supper. This recipe uses only half of a bread dough recipe, so you may make one loaf of whole-grain bread and two Spinach-Cheese Braids.

2 tablespoons olive oil
1 cup finely chopped onion
6 garlic cloves, minced
1 pound steamed fresh or thawed 10-ounce frozen spinach
$^{1}/_{4}$ cup grated Parmesan cheese
$^{3}/_{4}$ cup (3 ounces) grated mozzarella cheese

$^{1}/_{2}$ teaspoon salt
$^{1}/_{2}$ teaspoon pepper
Whole Grain Bread (page 68) prepared through the second rise
Oil or melted butter for brushing

Heat the oil in a large sauté pan or skillet over medium heat and sauté the onion and garlic until they are translucent, about 10 minutes. If using fresh spinach, rinse and place in a large saucepan over medium heat, cover, and cook for 2 or 3 minutes, or until wilted. Place the wilted fresh or the thawed spinach in a sieve or colander and press it with the back of a large spoon to remove as much moisture as possible. Add the spinach, Parmesan cheese, $^{1}/_{2}$ cup of the mozzarella, salt, and pepper to the onions and garlic.

Preheat the oven to 350°F. Roll out one-fourth of the bread dough into a rectangle approximately 8 by 16 inches and $^{1}/_{4}$-inch thick. Cut diagonal slices on each side of the dough, leaving a 3-inch strip uncut down the center of the dough. Spread half of the spinach filling down the center of the dough. Fold the diagonal slices over the top of the filling, in a braiding pattern, and fold up the ends to seal the dough and prevent the filling from running out while baking. Place on a lightly oiled baking sheet and top with half of the remaining grated mozzarella. Repeat with a second fourth of the dough and the remaining filling. Form the remaining dough into a loaf and bake as directed in the whole grain bread recipe.

Bake for 10 to 15 minutes, or until golden brown. Brush the loaves with oil or butter when you remove them from the oven. Serve immediately. To reheat, wrap loaves in foil and bake at 300°F for 15 minutes.

 Raisin Bread

Makes two 9-by-5-inch loaves

2¼ cups warm water
4 teaspoons (2 packages) active dried
   yeast
⅓ cup rolled oats
1 tablespoon salt
1 tablespoon ground cinnamon
¼ cup canola or other mild vegetable
   oil

6 tablespoon honey
1½ cups raisins
2¼ cups unbleached all-purpose flour
2¼ to 3 cups whole-wheat bread
   flour

Place warm water (should feel just warm on the inside of your wrist) in a large bowl. Stir in the yeast, oats, salt, cinnamon, oil, honey, and raisins with a wooden spoon. Add the unbleached all-purpose flour, 1 cup at a time, always stirring in the same direction. Stir the dough 100 times to develop the gluten. Stir in the whole-wheat flour 1 cup at a time until the dough becomes too stiff to stir with a spoon. Continue mixing in flour with your hand in the same direction until the dough pulls away from the sides of the bowl.

Turn the dough out onto a floured surface to knead. If any dough remains stuck in the bowl or on your hands, rub the sides of the bowl and your hands with a little flour and add these dough clumps to the other bread dough.

Follow the directions for kneading, first rise, and forming the dough into loaves in the recipe for whole-grain bread, page 68. Place the loaves in the prepared loaf pans and let it rise until doubled and rising over the top of the pans, about 1 hour. Preheat the oven to 375°F. Bake the bread for 40 minutes, or until golden brown. To test for doneness, remove a loaf from the pan and tap it on the bottom with your finger. If you hear a hollow sound, the loaves are done. Let cool on wire racks.

�֍ ▤ Whole Grain French Bread

Makes 3 small loaves

Our sourdough French bread from Upland Bakers is enormously popular. But since the amount of bread we buy is limited (they sell every loaf they make already and are not interested in enlarging their operation), we often run out. So, we began experimenting with our own French bread.

We began by making our bread out of only whole-wheat bread flour, but this gave us a very dense, flat bread. To lighten up the grain of the bread we began adding unbleached all-purpose flour in increasing amounts until we came up with a nutritional loaf that we could justifiably call French.

3 cups warm water (it should feel
   warm on the inside of your wrist)
4 teaspoons (2 packages) active dried
   yeast
1 tablespoon honey

3 teaspoons salt
1/2 cup raw wheat germ
2 cups whole-wheat bread flour
4 to 5 cups unbleached all-purpose
   flour

Mix the water, yeast, honey, salt, and wheat germ together in a large bowl. Add the whole-wheat flour and stir in one direction until it is completely mixed in, then stir 100 strokes in the same direction. Stir in the unbleached all-purpose flour 1 cup at a time in the same direction until you can't stir anymore. Rub the dough off the spoon with some of the flour and begin mixing the dough with your hands until it is not too sticky.

Turn the dough out onto a floured surface. If any dough remains in the bowl, put a little flour in and rub the sides of the bowl to get it off. Add this to your other dough. Knead the dough as described on page 68, adding the remaining flour a little at a time, until you have a very stiff dough that is not at all sticky and that springs back to its original shape when you press it with your finger.

Lightly oil a large bowl and place the dough in it. Turn the dough in the bowl to coat it with oil. Cover the dough with a cloth and let rise in a warm place until doubled, about 1 hour. Punch down the dough, knead it a few times, and divide the dough into 3 pieces. Shape the dough into rounds or logs and place them on baking sheets sprinkled with cornmeal. Cover and let rise in a warm place until almost doubled, about 1 hour.

Preheat the oven to 425°F. Make several diagonal slices across the top of the loaves with a sharp knife or razor blade, being careful not to crush or rip the dough. Moisten the loaves with a water mister or by brushing water onto them and place them in the oven. Bake for 20 minutes at 425°F, then reduce heat to 350°F and bake for 5 to 10 minutes more, or until golden brown. Let cool on wire racks.

❋ Whole–Grain Cinnamon Rolls

Makes 24 rolls

Dough

4$\frac{1}{2}$ cups warm water (just barely warm on the inside of your wrist)

2 tablespoons (3 packages) active dried yeast

$\frac{1}{4}$ cup canola or other mild vegetable oil

1$\frac{1}{2}$ cups honey

2 tablespoons salt

$\frac{1}{2}$ cup raw wheat germ

3$\frac{1}{2}$ to 4 cups unbleached all-purpose flour (with germ added back, if available)

3$\frac{1}{2}$ to 4 cups whole-wheat bread flour

* * *

Filling

$\frac{1}{2}$ cup (1 stick) butter, melted, or canola or other mild vegetable oil

3 to 4 tablespoons ground cinnamon

$\frac{1}{2}$ cup honey

$\frac{1}{2}$ cup (2 ounces) nuts (optional)

$\frac{1}{2}$ cup raisins (optional)

Stir the warm water, yeast, oil, honey, salt, and wheat germ in a large bowl. Stir in the unbleached all-purpose flour, 1 cup at a time, stirring always in the same direction. When the dough begins to stiffen but is not too stiff to stir comfortably, stir the dough 100 strokes in the same direction to develop the gluten. Add bread flour 1 cup at a time. Keep stirring until the dough pulls away from the sides of the bowl.

Turn the dough out onto a floured surface and knead the dough (see Whole Grain Bread, page 68, for kneading instructions) until it springs back slowly when you press it with your finger. Oil a large bowl, place the dough in the bowl, and turn the dough over to coat it with oil. Cover with a towel and let rise in a warm place, until doubled, about 1½ to 2 hours. Punch the dough down and turn it out onto a floured surface. Roll the dough out into a 16-by-20-inch rectangle ¼-inch thick. Brush generously with melted butter or oil. Sprinkle with cinnamon and honey, and nuts or raisins, if you like. Roll the dough into a log and cut it into 1-inch slices. Oil or butter two 9-by-13-inch baking dishes. Place the slices, cut-side down, into the prepared pans. Cover and let rise in a warm place until doubled in size, about 1 hour. About 20 minutes before baking, preheat the oven to 400°F. Bake the rolls for 15 minutes or until the tops are browned. Turn the rolls immediately out of the dishes onto plates.

❋ ▦ Whole-Wheat Tortillas

Makes twelve 8-inch tortillas

2 cups whole-wheat pastry flour
2 cups unbleached all-purpose flour
2 teaspoons baking powder
2 teaspoons salt

2 cups warm water
2 tablespoons canola or other mild
　vegetable oil

Mix the flours, baking powder, and salt together in a large bowl. Add 1 cup of the water and the oil and mix with a fork. Begin adding the remaining 1 cup of water a little at a time, while stirring, until the dough is moist and holds together but is not sticky. Turn the dough out onto a floured surface and knead it a few times, adding a little more flour if the dough is sticky or a little more water if it is too dry. Divide the dough into balls a little larger than 1 inch. Roll each ball out into an 8-inch circle, turning the dough frequently and rotating it to keep it round. Heat a dry griddle or large cast-iron skillet over medium-high heat and cook each tortilla until it begins to bubble on top, about 30 seconds. Turn the tortilla and cook the other side about 10 seconds more. Stack the tortillas and cover to keep them soft.

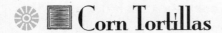 # Corn Tortillas

Makes 12 tortillas

I had never tried making corn tortillas before beginning this cookbook, mostly because I've never liked them. As it became necessary to use corn tortillas in some of our recipes, I began experimenting and found a recipe that I like.

1 cup corn flour
1 teaspoon salt
1 cup boiling water
2 teaspoons canola or other vegetable
   oil

1 to 1½ cups whole-wheat pastry flour
   or unbleached all-purpose flour

Place the corn flour and salt in a large bowl. Pour the boiling water over the flour and stir until all the dry ingredients are moistened. Let sit for a few minutes to allow the water to be absorbed. Mix in the oil and 1 cup of the wheat flour with a fork. Continue mixing in the flour until the dough is moist but not sticky. Turn out on a lightly floured surface and knead the dough with your hands for a few minutes, adding more flour if the dough seems sticky. Pinch off pieces of dough and form into 1-inch diameter balls.

Flatten one of the balls of dough with your hand. Turn the dough over and roll it with a rolling pin to flatten it more. Continue to roll and turn the dough, rotating the dough ¼ turn each time to help keep it round, until it is rolled into a 6-inch circle. Repeat for the remaining dough.

Heat a dry griddle or large cast-iron pan over medium-high heat and cook each tortilla for about 1 minute on the first side, or until bubbles begin to form. Flip the tortilla and cook for 30 seconds. Repeat to cook all of the tortillas. Serve immediately, or stack and wrap in a towel for later use.

Muffins

In all of our muffin recipes you may substitute 1 egg for each tablespoon of yogurt unless otherwise noted in the recipe. You should have the oven preheated and the muffin tins oiled or buttered and ready to go before you mix the wet and dry ingredients of the muffins together. If your muffins fall in the center when you take them out of the oven, it probably means that the oven wasn't hot enough or that the muffin batter was too thin. The batter should be thick enough that it drops off of the spoon into the muffin tin in one blob; it should not run or drip off of the spoon. If it is too thick, however, you should add more liquid or your muffins will be very dry. Muffins are done when a knife or toothpick inserted into the center of a muffin comes out dry. Let them cool in the pan for 5 minutes, then remove from tins.

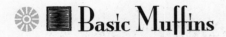 ## Basic Muffins

Makes 12 muffins

If you want to experiment with your own muffin variations, use this basic recipe.

3 cups whole-wheat pastry flour
1 tablespoon baking powder
1 teaspoon salt
½ cup plus 1 tablespoon honey
½ cup canola or other mild vegetable oil

3 tablespoons plain yogurt, or 3 eggs, beaten (if using eggs, reduce milk to 1 cup)
1¼ cups milk, plain soy milk, or fruit juice

* * *

Optional Ingredients

1/3 to 1/2 cup fresh fruit, dried fruit, or nuts

Ground nutmeg, cinnamon, cloves, or cardamom, to taste

Vanilla, almond, or other extracts, to taste

Preheat the oven to 400°F and oil 12 muffin tins. In a large bowl, combine the dry ingredients. In a medium bowl, mix the oil, honey, and yogurt. Add milk or other liquid. Stir the wet ingredients into the dry ingredients just until blended. Fill the prepared muffin tins two-thirds full and bake the muffins for 20 minutes, or until a toothpick inserted in the center of a muffin comes out dry. Let cool in the pan for 5 minutes, then remove from tins.

❋ Orange–Coconut Muffins

Makes 12 muffins

3 cups whole-wheat pastry flour

1 tablespoon baking powder

1/2 cup dried coconut

1 teaspoon salt

1/2 teaspoon ground cinnamon

1/4 teaspoon ground ginger

2/3 cup canola oil or other mild vegetable oil

1/2 cup honey

3 tablespoons plain yogurt, or 3 eggs, beaten (if using eggs, reduce milk to 3/4 cup)

2/3 cup orange juice

1 cup milk

1 tablespoon grated orange zest

Preheat the oven to 400°F and oil 12 muffin tins. Mix the dry ingredients together in a large bowl. In a medium bowl, stir the oil, honey, and yogurt or eggs together until they are well blended. Add the orange juice, milk, and zest. Add the wet to the dry ingredients and stir just until blended. Fill the prepared muffin tins two-thirds full and bake the muffins for 20 minutes, or until a toothpick inserted into the center of a muffin comes out clean. Let cool in the pan for 5 minutes, then remove from tins.

Egg- and Dairy-Free Orange-Coconut Muffins

Substitute 1¼ cups soy milk for the milk and yogurt in the above recipe.

✳ Maple–Corn Muffins

Makes 12 large muffins

This is one of our most popular muffins. We have a regular customer who calls or checks in frequently to see if we have Maple-Corn Muffins. When we have them, she buys extra and freezes them to tide her over until we bake them again.

2½ cups whole-wheat pastry flour
1½ cups cornmeal
4½ teaspoons baking powder
1 teaspoon salt
4 tablespoons plain yogurt, or 4 eggs,
    beaten (if using eggs, reduce milk
    to 1½ cups)

1¾ cups milk
¾ cup canola or other mild vegetable
    oil
½ cup maple syrup or honey

Preheat the oven to 400°F and oil or butter 12 muffin tins. Mix the dry ingredients together in a large bowl. In a medium bowl, stir the wet ingredients to blend well. Add the wet to the dry ingredients and stir just until blended. Fill the prepared muffin tins two-thirds full and bake for 20 minutes, or until a toothpick inserted in the center of a muffin comes out clean. Let cool in the pan for 5 minutes, then remove from tins.

Maple-Corn Blueberry Muffins

Follow the above recipe, but stir 1 cup fresh or frozen blueberries into the muffin batter before filling the tins.

✳ Blueberry Muffins

Makes 18 muffins

These were the first muffins we tried making without eggs. First we used tofu as an egg substitute, but we found that yogurt works much better.

4 cups whole-wheat pastry flour
4 teaspoons baking powder
1½ teaspoons salt
3 tablespoons plain yogurt, or 3 eggs, beaten (if using eggs, reduce milk to 1½ cups)

1¾ cups milk
¾ cup honey
½ cup canola or other mild vegetable oil
1 cup fresh or frozen blueberries

Preheat the oven to 400°F and oil 18 muffin tins. Mix the dry ingredients together in a large bowl. Mix the wet ingredients together in a separate bowl. Add milk. Mix the wet into the dry ingredients and stir until just blended. Add the blueberries and mix gently. Fill the muffin tins two-thirds full and bake for 20 minutes, or until a toothpick inserted into the center of a muffin comes out dry. Let cool in the pans for 5 minutes, then remove from tins.

EGG- AND DAIRY-FREE BLUEBERRY MUFFINS
Substitute 2 cups soy milk for the milk and yogurt in the above recipe.

✳ Molasses–Oat Muffins

Makes 18 muffins

3 cups whole-wheat pastry flour
1 cup unbleached all-purpose flour
1½ cups rolled oats

1 cup (4 ounces) chopped walnuts (optional)
4 teaspoons baking powder

1 teaspoon salt
1 teaspoon ground nutmeg
1 teaspoon ground cinnamon
2 teaspoons ground ginger
³/₄ cup canola or other mild vegetable
    oil

¹/₂ cup honey
¹/₂ cup molasses
4 tablespoons plain yogurt, or 4 eggs,
    beaten (if using eggs, reduce milk
    to 1³/₄ cup)
2 cups milk

Preheat the oven to 400°F and oil 12 muffin tins. Mix all the dry ingredients together in a large bowl. In a separate bowl, mix all of the wet ingredients together well. Stir the wet ingredients into the dry ingredients just until blended. Fill the prepared muffin tins two-thirds full and bake for 20 minutes, or until a toothpick inserted into the center of a muffin comes out clean. Let cool in the pan for 5 minutes, then remove from muffin tins.

❋ Apple–Rhubarb Muffins

Makes 18 muffins

4 cups whole-wheat pastry flour
4 teaspoons baking powder
1¹/₂ teaspoons salt
³/₄ cup canola or other mild vegetable
    oil
1 cup honey

4 tablespoons plain yogurt or 4 eggs,
    beaten (if using eggs, reduce milk
    to 1¹/₂ cups)
1³/₄ cups milk
1 cup ¹/₄-inch-diced apples
1 cup ¹/₄-inch-diced rhubarb

Preheat the oven to 400°F and oil 18 muffin tins. Mix the dry ingredients together in a large bowl. In a separate bowl, mix all the remaining ingredients except the apples and rhubarb. Stir the wet ingredients into the dry ingredients just until blended. Add the apples and rhubarb and stir just until they are evenly spread throughout the batter. Fill the prepared muffin tins two-thirds full and bake for 20 minutes, or until a toothpick inserted into the center of a muffin comes out dry. Let cool in the pan for 5 minutes, then remove from tins.

PEACH MUFFINS

Follow the above recipe for Apple-Rhubarb Muffins, but replace the apples and rhubarb with 2 cups $1/4$-inch-diced fresh peaches. Add 1 tablespoon ground cinnamon to the dry ingredients before combining the wet and dry ingredients.

❋ Cinnamon–Walnut Muffins

Makes 18 muffins

$4^1/4$ cups whole-wheat pastry flour
4 teaspoons baking powder
$1^1/2$ teaspoons salt
1 tablespoon ground cinnamon
3 tablespoons plain yogurt, or 3 eggs, beaten (if using eggs, reduce milk to 2 cups)

$3/4$ cup canola or other mild vegetable oil
$3/4$ cup honey
1 teaspoon vanilla extract
$2^1/4$ cups milk
1 cup (4 ounces) chopped walnuts

Preheat the oven to 400°F and oil 18 muffin tins. Mix all the dry ingredients together in a large bowl. In a medium bowl combine the oil, honey, yogurt, and vanilla and mix well. Add the milk. Combine the wet and dry ingredients and stir just until blended. Stir in the nuts until evenly distributed in the batter. Fill the prepared muffin tins two-thirds full and bake for 20 minutes, or until a toothpick inserted into a muffin comes out dry. Let cool in the pan for 5 minutes, then remove from tins.

❋ ▧ Raisin–Brown Rice Muffins

Makes 12 muffins

This egg- and dairy-free muffin is one of my favorites. We used to call them simply Brown Rice Muffins, which made them sound rather bland. Since we added the word *raisin* to the name, more people have ordered them.

2¹/₂ cups whole-wheat pastry flour
¹/₄ cup raw wheat germ
1 tablespoon baking powder
¹/₂ teaspoon salt
¹/₂ cup canola or other mild vegetable
    oil

²/₃ cup honey
1¹/₃ cups plain soy milk
1¹/₂ cups cooked brown rice

Preheat the oven to 400°F and oil 12 muffin tins. Mix the flour, wheat germ, baking powder, and salt together in a large bowl. Add the oil, honey, and soy milk to another large bowl and stir together until well blended. Stir in the rice. Mix the wet ingredients into the dry ingredients and stir just until mixed. Fill the prepared muffin tins two-thirds full and bake for 20 minutes, or until a toothpick inserted into a muffin comes out dry. Let cool in the pan for 5 minutes, then remove from tins.

GRANOLA MUFFINS
Substitute 1¹/₂ cups granola for the cooked rice and increase the soy milk to 1¹/₂ cups.

THREE-GRAIN MUFFINS
Substitute 1 cup rolled oats for 1 of the cups of cooked rice and increase the soy milk to 1¹/₂ cups.

 Pumpkin Muffins

Makes 12 muffins

In the fall, when fresh organic pumpkins are available, we cut small pie pumpkins in half and bake them on a baking sheet until the pumpkin is soft enough to scrape or squeeze out of the shell. Then we mash the pumpkin flesh slightly and use them to make these moist, spicy muffins. Canned pumpkin will work as well.

2¹/₂ cups whole-wheat pastry flour
1 tablespoon baking powder
1 teaspoon salt
1 teaspoon ground cinnamon
¹/₂ teaspoon ground ginger
¹/₄ teaspoon ground allspice
¹/₄ teaspoon ground cloves
1 cup cooked pumpkin
¹/₂ cup canola or other mild vegetable oil

²/₃ cup honey
2 tablespoons plain yogurt, or 2 eggs, beaten (if using eggs, reduce milk to 1¹/₄ cups)
1¹/₂ cups milk
¹/₂ cup (2 ounces) chopped walnuts or raisins

Preheat the oven to 400°F. Oil 12 muffin tins. Mix all the dry ingredients together in a large bowl. Mix the wet ingredients in a medium bowl. Add the wet to the dry ingredients and stir just until mixed. Stir in the nuts until evenly distributed. Fill muffin tins two-thirds full and bake for 20 minutes, or until a toothpick inserted into the center of a muffin comes out dry. Let cool in the pan for 5 minutes, then remove from tins.

❋ Spicy Pear Muffins

Makes 12 muffins

This is a moist, delicious muffin that's great in the fall, when local fresh pears are available.

3 cups whole-wheat pastry flour
1 tablespoon baking powder
¹/₂ teaspoon salt
1¹/₂ teaspoons ground cinnamon
³/₄ teaspoon ground nutmeg
³/₄ teaspoon ground ginger
³/₄ teaspoon ground cloves
¹/₂ cup canola or other mild vegetable oil

¹/₂ cup honey
2 tablespoons plain yogurt, or 2 eggs, beaten (if using eggs, reduce milk to 1¹/₄ cups)
1¹/₂ cups milk
2 small pears, cored, and chopped (1¹/₂ cups)

Preheat the oven to 400°F and oil 12 muffin tins. Mix the dry ingredients together in a large bowl. In a separate bowl, mix all the remaining ingredients, except the pears, together. Stir the wet ingredients into the dry ingredients just until just blended. Add the pears and stir to distribute them evenly. Fill the muffin tins two-thirds full and bake for 20 minutes, or until a toothpick inserted into a muffin comes out dry. Let cool in the pan for 5 minutes, then remove from muffin tins.

❋ Apple–Wheat Germ Muffins

Makes 12 muffins

We used to make these muffins using wheat bran. We tried using wheat germ to make them more nutritious and found that they also had a better flavor.

1 cup raw wheat germ
$2^3/_4$ cups whole-wheat pastry flour
1 tablespoon baking powder
$1^1/_2$ teaspoon ground cinnamon
1 teaspoon salt
$^1/_2$ cup plain yogurt

$1^3/_4$ to 2 cups milk
$^1/_2$ cup canola or other mild vegetable oil
$^2/_3$ cup honey
2 small apples, cored, and chopped ($1^1/_3$ cups)

Preheat the oven to 400°F and oil 12 muffin tins. Mix the dry ingredients together in a large bowl. Mix all the remaining ingredients, except the apples, in a medium bowl and stir well. Add the wet ingredients to the dry ingredients and mix just until blended. Stir in the apples to distribute evenly. Fill the muffin tins two-thirds full and bake for 20 minutes, or until a toothpick inserted into a muffin comes out dry. Let cool in the pan for 5 minutes, then remove from muffin tins.

Ginger Bran Muffins

Makes 16 muffins

We developed this recipe after we stopped using eggs in our muffins, so we've never made it with eggs. If you would like to try using eggs, refer to the previous muffin recipes and follow their directions.

2 cups whole-wheat pastry flour
2 cups unbleached all-purpose flour
1½ cups wheat bran
4 teaspoons baking powder
1 teaspoon salt
1 teaspoon ground nutmeg
1 teaspoon ground cinnamon
2 teaspoons ground ginger

¾ cup canola or other mild vegetable oil
½ cup honey
½ cup molasses
4 tablespoons plain yogurt
2¼ cups milk
1 cup (4 ounces) chopped walnuts or raisins

Preheat the oven to 400°F and oil 12 muffin tins. Mix the dry ingredients together in a large bowl. Mix the liquid ingredients together in another large bowl. Stir the wet into the dry ingredients until blended. Stir in the nuts or raisins just until evenly distributed. Fill the muffin tins two-thirds full and bake for about 20 minutes, or until a toothpick inserted in the center of a muffin comes out clean. Let cool in the pan for 5 minutes, then remove from muffin tins.

Desserts

DESSERTS ARE NOT A BIG PART of our business at the cafe, but we carry a fairly wide selection. We usually have an egg- and dairy-free offering, one dessert that is egg-free only, and an assortment of traditional desserts. Our desserts are almost always honey-sweetened. This doesn't mean that we are not occasionally chastised for not having more dairy- and egg-free, or fruit juice–sweetened, desserts. Although we have experimented with these kinds of sweets, they usually are just not as tasty as their less-nutritious counterparts. A case in point is our pumpkin pie recipe. We include two recipes in this cookbook. One is rich and delicious and always sells out. The other is egg- and dairy-free and is good, but it doesn't begin to compare in taste, although to dedicated vegans it is delicious.

Chocolate Chip Cookies

Makes 1 dozen large cookies

This is one of the few recipes in which we generally use white and brown sugar instead of natural sweeteners. Cookies made with honey tend to be more moist and break more easily than those made with sugar, and our customers prefer the sugar-sweetened version of these cookies over the honey-sweetened, egg-free version. We keep these cookies on hand regularly, and offer the eggless, honey-sweetened ones as an occasional option.

$^1/_2$ cup (1 stick) butter at room temperature

$^1/_2$ cup granulated sugar

$^1/_4$ cup packed brown sugar

1 egg, beaten

$^1/_2$ teaspoon vanilla extract

1$^3/_4$ cups whole-wheat pastry flour

$^1/_2$ teaspoon baking soda

$^1/_2$ teaspoon salt

1 teaspoon ground cinnamon

$^1/_4$ teaspoon ground nutmeg

$^3/_4$ cup (6 ounces) semisweet chocolate chips

$^1/_2$ cup (2 ounces) chopped walnuts

Preheat the oven to 375°F. Cream the butter and sugars together in a large bowl until fluffy. Stir in the beaten egg and vanilla until well blended.

Add all the remaining ingredients, except the chocolate chips and walnuts, in a separate bowl. Add this mixture to the butter and sugar mixture and mix well. Stir in the chocolate chips and walnuts until evenly mixed throughout the dough.

Drop by rounded tablespoonfuls onto an ungreased baking sheet. Press lightly with your hand to flatten. Bake for 10 minutes, or until lightly browned.

Honey-Sweetened Eggless Chocolate Chip Cookies

Follow the above recipe, but substitute $^3/_4$ cup honey for the granulated and brown sugars and 1 tablespoon yogurt for the egg. Increase the flour by $^1/_4$ cup. If you want to make this cookie totally sugar-free, use malt-sweetened chocolate chips instead of regular chocolate chips.

✳ Raspberry Shortbread

Makes 16 pieces

1$^1/_2$ cups (3 sticks) butter, at room temperature

$^3/_4$ cup Sucanat® or packed brown sugar

$^3/_4$ cup (3 ounces) chopped walnuts

3 cups whole-wheat pastry flour

1 cup raspberry preserves

1 to 2 tablespoons water

$^3/_4$ cup chocolate chips (optional)

Preheat the oven to 350°F. Cream the butter and Sucanat® or brown sugar together in a large bowl. Stir in the walnuts and flour until well blended. If the dough seems too thin, let it sit a few minutes to thicken. Press half of the dough into the bottom of a 9-by-13-inch baking pan and press down with the back of a spoon. In a small bowl, beat the raspberry preserves with the water to achieve a thick, pourable consistency and spread the mixture onto the dough. If you are adding chocolate chips, sprinkle them onto the preserves now. Crumble the remaining half of the dough on top and bake for 30 minutes, or until golden brown. Cut into 2-by-3-inch squares.

Cheesecake with Sour Cream Topping

Makes one 10-inch cheesecake

This recipe originated with my friend Hassan, whom I worked with many years ago in a large restaurant kitchen in Boulder, Colorado.

Filling

3 pounds cream cheese at room
   temperature
8 eggs
1¹/₂ cups honey

1 tablespoon vanilla extract
1 tablespoon lemon extract or grated
   lemon zest

❋ ❋ ❋

Crust

1¹/₂ packages (7¹/₂ ounces) graham
   crackers
6 tablespoons butter, melted

❋ ❋ ❋

Topping
14 ounces sour cream
2 tablespoons honey
1 tablespoon vanilla extract

Preheat the oven to 300°F. Combine all the filling ingredients in a large bowl or food processor and mix until smooth. *To make the crust:* Crush the graham crackers into fine crumbs with a rolling pin, a blender, or your hands. Place the crumbs in a medium bowl, add the melted butter, and mix well. Press the crumbs into the bottom and sides of a 10-inch springform pan. (If you don't have a springform pan, 2 pie pans will do.) Pour the filling into the crust and bake for about 1 hour. The cake is done when it has risen and the top looks firm and dry.

While the cake is baking, make the topping: Mix all the ingredients together in a small bowl. Remove the cake from the oven when done. Turn off the oven. Spread the topping onto the cheesecake and return it to the oven for 1 more hour, or until set.

 # Pineapple–Carrot Cake

Makes one 8-inch layer cake

An eggless, dairy-free carrot cake, made with tofu and whole-wheat flour.

1½ cups whole-wheat pastry flour
1½ cups unbleached all-purpose flour
1 cup flaked dried coconut
1 tablespoon baking powder
1 tablespoon ground cinnamon
1 teaspoon salt
¾ cup canola or other mild vegetable oil
2 teaspoons vanilla extract

2 teaspoons grated orange zest
1½ cups honey
One 16-ounce can of crushed, unsweetened pineapple in water, or 2 cups fresh, finely chopped pineapple (if using fresh pineapple, you will need up to ½ cup additional liquid—either soy milk or fruit juice)

8 ounces firm tofu
4 carrots, grated (2 cups)
Honey-Nut Frosting (recipe follows)

Preheat the oven to 350°F. Brush two 8-inch round cake pans with oil and dust with flour. Mix the dry ingredients together in a large bowl. In a blender or food processor, blend together all the other ingredients, except the carrots, until smooth. Stir the wet ingredients into the dry ingredients. Fold in the carrots just until evenly distributed throughout batter. Pour half of the batter into each pan and bake for 20 to 25 minutes, or until the cake is golden and a toothpick inserted into the center comes out dry.

Let the cakes cool completely in the pans. Shake each cake gently to see if it will come out of the pan easily. If it seems to be sticking, gently insert a spatula or a flexible knife under the cake to loosen it. Spread about one-fourth of the frosting on top of one cake. Place the other cake on top of the frosted cake. Using a wide knife, spread the remaining frosting on the top and sides of the cake.

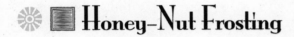 Honey–Nut Frosting

*Makes enough frosting for
one 8-inch 2-layer cake*

1¹/₂ cups (6 ounces) walnuts
1¹/₂ cups (6 ounces) almonds (or
   3 cups of either walnuts or
   almonds)

2 cups flaked dried coconut
³/₄ to 1 cup plain soy milk
1 cup honey
1 teaspoon vanilla extract

Place the nuts on a baking sheet in a preheated 350°F oven for 5 to 8 minutes, or until lightly toasted, being careful not to burn them. Blend the nuts, coconut, ³/₄ cup of the soy milk, the honey and vanilla in a blender or food processor. Add the remaining soy milk as necessary to make a frosting of spreading consistency.

❁ Maple–Walnut Coffee Cake

Makes one 9-by-13-inch cake

I remember this recipe from my childhood. It is still one of my favorites, although we now make it without the eggs and white sugar that my mother used.

Cake

4 cups whole-wheat pastry flour
1 tablespoon baking powder
1 teaspoon baking soda
1½ teaspoons salt
1½ teaspoons ground cinnamon

¾ cup canola or other mild vegetable oil
½ cup plain yogurt
1 cup maple syrup or honey
1½ cups milk

❊ ❊ ❊

Topping

¼ cup whole-wheat pastry flour
3 tablespoons Sucanat® or packed brown sugar
¼ teaspoon ground cinnamon

1 tablespoon canola or other mild vegetable oil
1 cup (4 ounces) walnuts, chopped

To make the cake: Preheat the oven to 350°F and grease a 9-by-13-inch baking pan. Mix the dry ingredients together thoroughly in a large bowl. Mix the oil, yogurt, and maple syrup or honey together in a medium bowl until smooth. Stir in the milk. Add the wet ingredients to the dry ingredients and stir just to mix. Pour the batter into the prepared pan.

    To make the topping: Mix the flour, Sucanat® or brown sugar, cinnamon, and oil together in a small bowl. Sprinkle this mixture over the top of cake, then sprinkle the walnuts on top. Bake for 45 minutes, or until a toothpick inserted in the middle of the cake comes out dry.

❋ Strawberry Shortcake

Serves 6

We make this dessert in early July, when local, organic strawberries are available. Unfortunately, this is for only a few weeks, so we serve the same shortcake with other fresh fruits and berries, such as raspberries, blackberries, and sliced peaches.

Shortcake

1 cup whole-wheat pastry flour
1 cup unbleached all-purpose flour
4 teaspoons baking powder
1/2 teaspoon salt
6 tablespoons cold butter

4 tablespoons plain yogurt
3 tablespoons maple syrup or honey
2 teaspoons vanilla extract
1/2 cup milk or more as needed

❋ ❋ ❋

2 cups fresh strawberries, stemmed and sliced
2 tablespoons honey

1 cup heavy (whipping) cream
1/2 teaspoon vanilla or almond extract
1 to 2 tablespoons maple syrup

To make the shortcake: Preheat the oven to 400°F. Mix the dry ingredients together in a medium bowl. Cut the butter into the dry ingredients using a pastry cutter, or shred it into the flour mixture using the large holes of a grater. Mix the butter gently into the flour. Mix the yogurt, maple syrup or honey, and vanilla together until the yogurt is smooth and the sweetener is well blended in. Blend in the 1/2 cup milk and pour the wet ingredients into the dry ingredients. Stir with a fork just until the dough sticks together. If the mixture is too dry, add milk in very small increments just until the dough is moistened and sticking together. Knead the dough a few times in the bowl until all of the flour has been incorporated and it is smooth. Roll the dough out on a lightly floured surface to a thickness of 3/4-inch and cut out circles with a 2 1/2-inch biscuit cutter. Place the biscuits on an ungreased baking sheet and bake for 10 to 12 minutes, or until golden brown. Remove from the oven and set aside to cool.

Mix the strawberries and honey together. In a deep bowl, beat the cream, vanilla, and maple syrup together until soft peaks form. Cut the shortcake biscuits in half crosswise. Spoon half of the strawberries onto the bottom half of each biscuit and top with half of the whipped cream. Place the top half of each biscuit on the whipped cream and spoon some of the remaining strawberries and whipped cream on top. Serve immediately.

 Rice Pudding

Makes 4 servings

An egg- and dairy-free pudding made with soy milk and brown rice.

3 cups cooked brown rice ($1^{1}/_{2}$ cups dry)
2 cups plain soy milk
1 teaspoon vanilla extract
$^{1}/_{2}$ teaspoon ground cinnamon

$^{1}/_{4}$ teaspoon ground nutmeg
$^{1}/_{2}$ teaspoon freshly grated lemon or orange zest
$^{1}/_{3}$ cup honey
$^{1}/_{2}$ cup raisins

Preheat the oven to 350°F. Mix all ingredients together in an 8-by-8-inch square baking dish. Bake for 10 minutes, then stir thoroughly and return to the oven for 10 minutes. Stir again and bake for another 10 minutes. Let cool. (NOTE: A skin will probably develop on top of the pudding while it is baking. Either remove this before you stir or simply mix it in.)

Pumpkin Pie

Makes one 10-inch pie

We begin baking pumpkin pies in the fall as soon as organic pie pumpkins are available. We cut the pumpkins in half lengthwise, scoop out the seeds and membranes, and bake them facedown at 375°F in ¹/₂-inch of water on baking sheets. They are done when the skin gives way when you push on it, about 45 minutes. When pumpkins are no longer available, we substitute other winter squashes, with excellent results. We freeze any pumpkin that we don't use immediately and save it to make pies during the winter.

1 10-inch pie crust (page 99)
4 eggs, beaten
3 cups cooked pumpkin (your own
  or canned)
²/₃ cup honey
³/₄ teaspoon salt

1¹/₂ teaspoons ground cinnamon
³/₄ teaspoon ground ginger
¹/₂ teaspoon ground allspice
¹/₂ teaspoon ground cloves
1¹/₄ cups heavy (whipping) cream

Preheat the oven to 375°F. Mix all the ingredients together in a blender or large bowl until smooth and creamy. Pour into the pie shell. Bake for 45 to 55 minutes, or until the top begins to crack.

EGG- AND DAIRY-FREE PUMPKIN PIE

Substitute 8 ounces mashed tofu (1 cup) for the eggs and 1 cup soy milk for the cream. Add 3 tablespoons arrowroot and mix all together in a blender or food processor until smooth. Use the dairy-free pie crust recipe on page 100. Bake for 30 to 40 minutes, or until top begins to crack.

Orange Pecan Pie

Makes one 10-inch pie

$1/2$ cup Sucanat® or packed brown sugar

$1/2$ cup (1 stick) butter, at room temperature

4 eggs

$1/2$ cup maple syrup

$1/2$ cup honey

3 tablespoons Grand Marnier or other orange liqueur

2 teaspoons grated orange zest

2 cups (8 ounces) pecan halves

One 10-inch pie shell

Preheat the oven to 375°F. In a large bowl, beat the Sucanat® or brown sugar with the butter until fluffy. Beat in the eggs one at a time, then blend in the maple syrup, honey, liqueur, and zest. Pour this mixture into the pie shell. Sprinkle the pecans evenly over the pie filling—they will sink as it bakes. Bake for 5 minutes at 375°F, then reduce heat to 325°F and bake for an additional 45 minutes, or until crust is golden brown.

 # Rhubarb Pie

Makes one 10-inch pie

Rhubarb has a short season in late spring, so while it is in season, we use a lot of it in pies and muffins. Rhubarb mixes well with other fruits, such as strawberries, peaches, apples, or blueberries.

8 stalks rhubarb, cut into 1-inch pieces (8 cups)

$1^{1}/4$ cups honey

$1/2$ cup whole-wheat pastry flour

5 tablespoons arrowroot or cornstarch

$1^{1}/2$ teaspoons fresh orange or fresh lemon juice

1 tablespoon grated orange or lemon zest

1 recipe Pie Crust (page 99) or
    Dairy-Free Pie Crust (page 100)

Preheat the oven to 425°F. Combine the rhubarb, honey, flour, arrowroot or cornstarch, juice, and zest in a large bowl and mix well. Roll out the bottom pie crust and fit it into a 10-inch-pan as directed in the recipe. Fill it with the rhubarb filling. Roll out the top crust and place it over the filling. Seal and flute as described on page 100. Cut several slits in the top crust to allow steam to escape. Bake at 425°F for 10 minutes, then reduce the temperature to 325°F and bake for 35 minutes more, or until the crust is golden.

VARIATIONS
Replace half of the rhubarb with strawberries, blueberries, peaches, apples, or other fruit. Reduce the honey to 1 cup.

 # Pie Crust

Makes one 10-inch, 2-crust pie

1½ cups whole-wheat pastry flour   ⅔ cup (1⅓ stick) cold butter
1½ cups unbleached all-purpose flour   ½ cup milk
Pinch of salt

Place the flours and salt in a medium bowl. Using a pastry cutter or 2 knives, cut the butter into the flour, or grate the butter into the flour using the large holes of a grater. Gradually mix in the milk with a fork, until the dough holds together well; you may not need all of the milk. Don't overmix the dough. Divide the dough in half and roll out each piece on a lightly floured surface, turning the dough over and rotating it ¼ turn each time you roll it, so that the finished dough is relatively round and about 2 inches larger across than the top of the pie pan.

    Fit the rolled dough into the pie pan, making sure that it is pressed snugly up against the pan all the way around. If you are making a 2-crust pie, cut the dough off at the outer edge of the pie pan with a knife. If you are making a single-crust pie, trim the dough with scissors to about ¹/₂-inch larger than the outside edge of the pie pan, fold the extra dough under, and flute the edge (see the following paragraph).

Roll out the second crust and place it over the filling in the pie. With scissors, trim the dough about ¹/₂-inch larger than the pie pan. Fold the top crust under the bottom crust, as for a single-crust pie. Press the dough firmly against the flat rim of the pie pan with one hand, using the other hand to keep the dough even with the edge of the pie pan. This will seal the crusts together. To make a fluted edge, use the thumb of your right hand to push the dough between the thumb and index finger of your left hand. Keep moving your left hand around the crust, placing your thumb into the groove created previously, until you have gone all around the crust.

❋ ▣ Dairy–Free Pie Crust

Makes one 10-inch, 2-crust pie

Most dairy-free pie crusts tend to fall apart when you roll them out. This one is not as flaky as crusts using butter, but it is the best dairy-free recipe we've found.

1¹/₂ cups whole-wheat pastry flour
1¹/₂ cups unbleached all-purpose flour
¹/₂ teaspoon salt

4 tablespoons canola or other mild vegetable oil
³/₄ cups cold plain soy milk or water

Combine the flours, salt, and oil together in a medium bowl. Add the soy milk or water and mix with a fork until the flours are fully moistened. Knead briefly with your hands to complete mixing. Separate the dough into 2 equal pieces and roll out on a lightly floured surface as directed in the preceding recipe.

Mini Mongrels

My nine-year-old son Ethan coined this name for a dessert snack my wife makes with leftover pie crust dough. Roll the dough out to a thickness of $1/8$ inch. Sprinkle it generously with cinnamon and honey or sugar. Roll it up into a roll and cut it into 1-inch slices. Bake on a baking sheet or pie pan in a preheated 350°F oven for about 10 minutes, or until lightly browned.

Drinks

SOME OF THE DRINKS THAT WE OFFER at the cafe are seasonal, such as lemonade and iced teas and coffees. We used to serve hot chocolate only in the winter but have found that it is popular year-round, especially for children at breakfast. Here are some of our recipes for refreshing beverages.

Fruit Juice Spritzers

Makes 1 serving

We serve canned fruit juice spritzers as a healthful alternative to other kinds of soda. But when we don't have a certain flavor, we make our own.

Ice cubes
$^3/_4$ glass fruit juice (any kind or
    mixture)
$^1/_4$ glass carbonated spring water

Add ice cubes to a glass. Pour the fruit juice into the glass, add spring water, and stir.

Lemonade

Makes ¹/₂ gallon

1³/₄ cups fresh lemon juice (about
    7 lemons)
¹/₂ cup honey

2 cups hot water
4 cups cold water

Pour the lemon juice into a ¹/₂-gallon pitcher. Mix the honey with the hot water until it is completely dissolved and add it to the lemon juice. Add the cold water to the pitcher and stir. Serve over ice.

LIMEADE
Substitute lime juice for lemon juice in the above recipe.

Hot Chocolate Mix

Makes 5 ¹/₂ cups mix

The mix stores well, so you can have a ready supply for future use.

1 cup unsweetened cocoa powder
3 cups dried milk
1¹/₂ cups Sucanat® or packed brown
    sugar

Combine the cocoa powder, dried milk, and Sucanat® and mix well. Store in a tightly sealed container, such as a recycled, quart-sized yogurt container.

HOT CHOCOLATE

Place $1/2$ cup mix in each 10-ounce mug or $1/3$ cup in each 8-ounce cup. Add hot water to fill the mug or cup. Top with whipped cream if you have it. A sprinkle of cinnamon on top is also nice.

MOCHACCINO

Replace the hot water in the preceding recipe with hot coffee.

Fruit and Yogurt Drink

Makes 2 servings

$1/2$ cup plain yogurt
$1/2$ cup fruit juice (we generally use
   apple or apple-strawberry)

2 cups mixed chopped fruits and/or
   berries
Ice cubes (optional)

Place the yogurt, juice, and fruit in a blender and blend until smooth. Add ice cubes to make the drink very cold.

Index